Working with Animals

Working with Animals

*An exciting guide to opportunities
and training in this rewarding vocation*

ALEX GOUGH

How To Books

Published by How To Books Ltd,
3 Newtec Place, Magdalen Road,
Oxford OX4 1RE, United Kingdom.
Tel: (01865) 793806. Fax: (01865) 248780.
email: info@howtobooks.co.uk
www.howtobooks.co.uk

British Library Cataloguing in Publication Data
A catalogue record for this book is available from
the British Library.

Edited by Diana Brueton
Cover design by Shireen Nathoo Design
Cover image PhotoDisc

Produced for How To Books by Deer Park Productions
Typeset by Anneset, Weston-super-Mare, N Somerset
Printed and bound by Cromwell Press, Trowbridge, Wiltshire.

NOTE: The material contained in this book is set out in good
faith for general guidance and no liability can be accepted
for loss or expense incurred as a result of relying in particular
circumstances on statements made in the book. Laws and
regulations are complex and liable to change, and readers should
check the current position with the relevant authorities before
making personal arrangements.

Contents

List of Illustrations

Preface

Working with animals entails hard work, low pay, long hours and can be distressing. It also brings job satisfaction, excitement, mental and physical challenges and joy. Nine people in various animal-orientated careers were interviewed for this book and, despite many gripes and moans, not one would alter their career options if they were able to choose again. This shows what a hold working with animals can have over people's lives, and how much they are prepared to put up with to continue doing the job they love.

My personal experience confirms this. In my time spent training to be a veterinary surgeon I worked in a variety of jobs, from lambing sheep and milking cows, to a short stint as a veterinary nurse. I enjoyed all the jobs I did, and the people I worked with were by and large content. This, despite feelings of under-appreciation and low pay from veterinary nurses, poor market conditions for farmers and high stress levels in vets.

Something makes working with animals special, and the obvious conclusion is that it is the animals themselves that make it so. It is the love of the animals that sends the farmer out milking at 4 am, the vet attending a cat involved in a road accident at midnight and the zoo keeper mucking out the elephants!

Of course, working with animals is not for everyone, and if you are unsure, this book should help you make up your mind. But if you still don't know if a job with animals is for you, try it and see. If there is one thing I have emphasised in this book, it is the need to gain work experience. If you decide you don't like it, time spent gaining experience with animals still looks good on most CVs. But many people will be hooked for life.

I would like to take this opportunity to thank all the people who have assisted with this book: those who contributed for the case studies, those organisations which provided useful information; and How To Books for bringing it all to fruition.

Alex Gough

1

Careers with Animals

WHY WORK WITH ANIMALS?

If you are reading this book, you are considering a career working with animals. Before you go any further, this is a good time to examine your motives.

First, what do most people look for in a job? The priorities are different for different people, but they boil down to several important factors:

- job satisfaction

- job security

- good working conditions

- reasonable hours

- good pay.

What order of importance would you put them in? If it is roughly as above, then a career with animals may be right for you. Working with animals can be immensely satisfying, and with the possible exception of the agriculture industry, the numbers of domesticated animals in the country show no signs of declining. This suggests that jobs working with animals will always be available.

However, if you are more interested in good pay and short hours, it might be worth reconsidering. Domestic animals often need care around the clock, and have no respect for the hour when needing your attention. If you are a farmer, a stable hand or a veterinary nurse, expect to work unsociable hours, at least some of the time.

As for pay, it is a sad fact that people are only prepared to spend a limited amount on their animals. To a farmer, this is a simple matter of economics, to a pet owner it will depend on their personal resources. The consequence of this is that although a huge amount of money is spent on animals per year, if looked at per head of animal, this figure is actually quite low compared to the amount of time and energy it takes to provide a service for that animal.

Job conditions are highly variable, from the cosy corner pet shop to the cold, wet hill farm. In this area you have more choice, depending on your constitution and the degree of hardship you are prepared to put up with.

So if pay and hours, and sometimes conditions, are so poor, why do so many people work with animals? There are a variety of reasons, including:

- Enjoying caring for animals.

- Being good at some aspect of working with animals.

- Desiring to help animals and/or their owners.

- Enjoying competing with animals.

- Wanting to work outdoors.

It is certainly true, as you will find from reading the case studies in the subsequent chapters, that for many working with animals is its own reward. That sometimes you can get paid for it is often just an added bonus.

WHAT WORKING WITH ANIMALS ENTAILS

Flicking through this book will show you the huge variety of jobs with animals available, and their pay, working conditions and duties are tremendously diverse. However, there are some things that the majority have in common. Most involve some degree of contact with animals and animal handling. In most cases you will take responsibility for individual or groups of animals at certain times. This means that you must look out for their health and welfare, as well as working with them to perform specific tasks. You will develop skills that help you decide when an animal is not performing as it should, or is unwell. The animals in your care will rely on you for food, water, attention to basic health problems and seeking of veterinary attention when required, shelter, and various other needs which vary from species to species.

Working with the owners

Another important part of many jobs with animals is working with the people who own them. Whether this is the farmer, whose livestock are his livelihood, or the old lady whose Yorkshire terrier is her only companion, you will need to talk to these people to explain what you are doing, and persuade them that you are sufficiently skilled at your job to perform it with competence. Many owners will have made a significant emotional investment in their animals, and they must always be treated with tact and consideration.

WHAT QUALITIES YOU NEED

Different careers working with animals require different skills and attributes, but certain qualities are required by the majority of animal careers. These include:

- having a caring attitude

- being dedicated to your job

- having good interpersonal skills

- having good practical skills

- being hard working.

Another requirement that varies is your academic ability, with some jobs needing no formal qualifications, while others require the highest levels of school and university education. Requirements for physical strength and fitness also vary, being naturally important for working in the armed forces or as a farrier, but obviously far less so for the person running a boarding cattery.

It is important that you do not delude yourself as to your own personal qualities. Not only must you convince your potential employer that you are up to the job, but you must then go on to do the job on a daily basis. If you are ill-equipped for the task, for reasons of lack of academic ability, lack of fitness or lack of motivation for example, not only will you do the job badly, disappointing your employers and potentially causing suffering to the animals, but you will gain no enjoyment or satisfaction from the job yourself. And remember, very few people work with animals for the money. Most could probably earn more elsewhere.

HOW TO GAIN EXPERIENCE

Gaining experience of working with animals is vital to anyone interested in a career in this area. There are several reasons why experience is so important:

● By gaining experience, you find out if you are capable of doing the job.

● By gaining experience, you find out if you enjoy doing the job.

● The more experience you have, the easier it will be to get a job.

● If you decide that the job is for you, your experience will make you better at the job, more confident, and your first week far less nerve-wracking.

Different levels of experience are required for different animal careers. Sometimes rules are laid down by examining bodies regarding minimum requirements (eg veterinary surgeons – see Chapter 2). In other cases the amount of experience needed will be largely up to you. But the basic rule is the same: the more the better.

If you are currently in full-time education or employment then it may seem difficult to fit work experience in. But remember that animal care is a 24-hour business, and it is often in evenings and at weekends that people working with animals appreciate some voluntary help. Also, make good use of your holidays to gain experience. Commitment and dedication are important in animal careers, and it is never too early to start demonstrating these qualities.

Finding a work experience placement

Now the question arises of how to find a suitable placement. If you are at school or university, then teachers and careers advisers can often help. Don't turn your nose up at personal contacts – if your uncle owns a farm and your interest is in agriculture, then spend some time working with him. He is likely to be far more patient with you and teach you more than a relative stranger.

If you have no personal contacts, and no help from careers professionals, then you must do some research. The best place to start is the *Yellow Pages*. A reasonably sized business might have an official policy on accepting work experience students, but a smaller one may also be glad to help. Try to get a placement shadowing the type of job in which you are interested. If this is difficult though, for example if there is nothing suitable in your location, find somewhere that deals with the species you want to work with. For instance, if you want to work as a veterinary nurse, experience in a boarding kennels may help. Initial contact by phone is preferable – you can usually get a much quicker yes or no, and ask or answer any questions that crop up. However, sometimes it can be hard to get an answer or speak to someone who can make a decision, in which case a letter (see Figure 1) is appropriate. Other things to look out for and note when seeking a placement or doing work experience are listed below:

● Working with animals can be dangerous. Make sure that your place of work experience includes you in their insurance policy for personal injury. You can also check with your school, if your experience is arranged this way. If you do not have cover, you should seriously consider organising some yourself.

● Do some research before deciding where to go. How often do they take students? Will you be there on your own and so get personal attention, or will there be several of you? Will you be permitted to do anything, or will you only be allowed to watch? (NB – in veterinary practices you may not be allowed much physical contact with the animals for insurance reasons.)

23 March 200X

Jason Brown
The Old Vicarage
Little Nottley
Northshire
NX7 2BB
0111 8765433

Dear Sir/Madam,

I am currently in year 10 at school, and am considering a career in agriculture. I am writing to enquire whether it would be possible to come to your farm for a period of one week in my school holidays, preferably the week beginning the 5th or 12th of April, to gain experience of farm work.

I have very little experience with farm animals, but I am willing to work hard and get my hands dirty. Naturally, I will not be expecting any pay.

I look forward to hearing from you. I enclose a stamped addressed envelope for your convenience.

Yours sincerely,

Jason Brown

Fig. 1. Sample letter 1 – application for work experience placement.

● Bear in mind that places of work experience have no obligation to take you, and get no pay for so doing. Help to make your placement pleasant for all concerned by being punctual, helpful, cheerful and well-presented.

● Places of work can get very busy. Don't be offended if you don't get much attention. Offer to help, but don't be pushy.

● Ask questions. It is far more rewarding for the person you are shadowing to feel you are interested, than if you follow them around in silence with a long face. They will then in turn be more helpful towards you.

● Don't expect to be paid. You will usually be more hindrance than help!

HOW TO GET A JOB

Once you have decided which career you want to embark on, and you have got the appropriate academic qualifications, it is time to start looking. More details of the specifics of this process can be found later in the book under different job descriptions. However, there are certain generalisations which hold true for the job hunting process.

Finding a vacancy

The first step is to find a vacancy. For certain careers the professional magazines will be the first place to look, for example the *Veterinary Record* for vets and nurses (published by the British Veterinary Association, see Useful Addresses at the end of Chapter 2). Other less specialist jobs, such as kennel assistant or stable hand, may be advertised locally. Check the jobs sections of local papers, adverts on shop windows, and employment agencies and job centres.

Another way to find a job is to write on spec to different businesses that appeal to you. Sending a CV is optional at this stage. If yours is particularly impressive it may help, but an initial enquiry letter, such as the one in Figure 2 should be sufficient. The majority will probably come back saying they have no vacancies, but many will keep you on file should a position arise. By the law of averages, the bigger the business and the more people

23 March 200X

Jane Smith
The Bungalow
Little Nottley
Northshire
NX7 2BA
0111 8765432

Dear Sir/Madam,

I have just left school, and intend to pursue a career as a veterinary nurse. I am writing to enquire whether you have any positions available for a trainee nurse, either now or in the near future.

I am 18 years old, and have two A levels and six GCSEs. I have previously spent two weeks gaining work experience at Bloggs and Bloggs Veterinary Surgery in Little Nottley, and have worked for the last six months as a kennel hand at a local boarding kennels. I have a CV available. Please phone or write if you require any further information.

I look forward to hearing from you. I enclose a stamped addressed envelope for your convenience.

Yours sincerely.

Jane Smith

Fig. 2. Sample letter 2 – 'on spec' job application.

they employ, the more likely they are to have a vacancy. If you are lucky you may get one or more replies. This method of job-hunting has the advantage that you can jump the queue. Often you will be interviewed first, before the job is advertised, and if they like you they may not bother going to the expense and inconvenience of advertising, but offer you the job. Even if they do still advertise, you are more likely to be memorable for having shown the enthusiasm and initiative to apply off your own back.

Applying with a CV
Once you have found a vacancy that you like the look of, you should apply in writing with a CV. Your cover letter should state your interest in the job, and briefly outline your qualifications and experience, and why you consider yourself suited to the job. The details should be in your CV – keep the cover letter short and to the point.

There are many books on the subject of writing a CV, but the information you should include is:

- full name

- current address

- marital status

- driving licence held

- secondary and tertiary education

- academic qualifications

- previous employment

- relevant experience

- hobbies and interests.

You can also include a paragraph on your personal qualities. Take the time to produce a professional-looking CV. Pay attention to details such as presentation and spelling – if there are a lot of candidates of similar ability these things make a difference.

Being interviewed

If your CV interests your potential employer you will probably be invited for an interview. This is not only an opportunity for the interviewers to assess you, but for you to assess them. Ask to look around the premises, and have a list of questions ready, such as pay, holiday, prospects, on the job training etc. Be punctual, smart and answer questions fully (not with one-word answers). Look your interviewer in the eye and try to relax. Some nervousness is understandable, so don't panic if you trip over your words. However, if you know or fear that you will get extremely anxious in an interview, then relaxation exercises before can help greatly.

USEFUL ADDRESSES AND WEB SITES

Animal Information Bureau, Unit 4, Telford Court, Little Mead Industrial Estate, Cranleigh, Surrey GU6 8ND. Tel: (01483) 273964.

Careers and Occupational Information Centre, PO Box 298a, Thames Ditton, Surrey KT7 0ZS,

Career World UK: www.careerworld.net (general careers advice).

Career Solutions: www.careersolutions.co.uk/index.html (general careers advice and CV writing tips).

City and Guilds, 1 Giltspur Street, London EC1A 9DD. www.city-and-guilds.co.uk

Colin Seymour's Brief Guide to Writing a CV: www.users.dircon.co.uk/netking/cvskel.htm.

Universities Federation for Animal Welfare, 8 Hamilton Close, South Mimms, Potters Bar, Hertfordshire EN6 3QD. Tel: (01707) 658202.

FURTHER READING

Careers Working with Animals, Allan Shepherd (Kogan Page).

Occupations 2000, Ed. J Leavesley (Department for Education and Employment).

2

The Veterinary Professions

This chapter examines the professions that deal with animal health problems and diseases, namely:

● veterinary surgeon

● veterinary nurse.

VETERINARY SURGEON

Job description
Vets can work with all species of animals, although many choose to specialise in a narrower range, such as pets, horses or farm animals. By law only properly qualified vets may practice veterinary medicine and surgery in this country. This means that only vets may diagnose and treat diseases in animals, and only vets may perform surgery on animals. There are some exceptions to this last rule, however. Veterinary nurses may perform minor surgery under the supervision of a vet, and researchers in possession of a Home Office licence may also perform certain types of surgery for research purposes.

To practise as a vet in this country, it is necessary to be a Member of the Royal College of Veterinary Surgeons (MRCVS). Entry into this body is by way of a qualifying degree, such as the Bachelor of Veterinary Medicine (see The Veterinary Course). On admission to the Royal College all vets take an oath, that 'my constant endeavour will be to uphold the welfare of animals in my care.'

There are a number of career options open to the veterinary graduate.

General practice

The majority of vets work in general practice. There are still many jobs available in mixed practise dealing with all domestic species (the typical 'James Herriot' practice). However, with a greater degree of specialisation, and the decline in agriculture in this country, it may become harder to find a job in mixed practice.

In the mixed practice the vet may start the day consulting (appointments or open surgery), where he or she deals with all manner of problems in dogs, cats, rabbits, small mammals, and sometimes reptiles and birds. After consulting it might be time to operate. Veterinary surgeons are expected to perform all sorts of operations, from minor neutering and stitch-ups, to major gastrointestinal surgery or internal fixation of broken bones. In addition, the modern vet will work with a great deal of sophisticated monitoring and diagnostic equipment such as x-ray machines, ECG monitors, ultrasound, and blood haematology and biochemistry analysers.

After lunch, if there has been time to eat any, the vet may need to go out on visits to farm animals and horses. Obviously it is difficult or impossible for the larger animals to be brought to the surgery, so it is necessary to drive to them. Often pet owners will request a visit too, if an animal is too ill to move, or the owner is housebound. A car is usually provided by the practice for personal and professional use; alternatively if the vet's own car is used, the practice may pay a petrol allowance.

The structure of the day

The working day usually finishes at 6 to 7 o'clock, but there is a legal and ethical obligation on veterinary practices to provide emergency cover 24 hours a day, 365 days a year. Some small animal practices in cities form co-operatives with other practices or use specialist emergency practices to cover the out-of-normal-hours work. Most practices find this too expensive or impractical, however, and it is more common for the vets in one practice to take it in turns to cover emergency work in the evenings, at weekends and on bank holidays. This is known as being 'on call' or 'on duty.' So if you work in a five-vet practice, you will be on call one evening and one weekend out of every five. While being in a three-vet practice might seem like your on-call rota will be that much harder, you are less likely to be called out in a smaller practice.

So if it is a vet's evening on call, he or she will have to be available to attend emergencies, for example if an anxious farmer calls you out to help a cow that is having a difficult calving. Even if they spend most of the evening performing a caesarean section on it, they are still on duty when they get home, and the phone may still ring at any time. And come 9 o'clock the next morning, they will be back at work. Some practices give the next day or morning off, but the majority will expect a full day's work, possibly with a half-day's holiday later in the week to compensate.

The structure of the working day will vary considerably from practice to practice, depending on workload, species dealt with, and personal preferences of the practice partners.

Research
There is a sizeable number of vets engaged in scientific research. The main employers for vets who wish to pursue a research career are the universities and the pharmaceutical companies. Often the universities will expect a candidate to be studying for, or already possess, a PhD, and there may be an expectancy to publish scientific papers. Subjects for research at universities can be quite obscure and not of obvious immediate benefit (although this sort of basic research is often vital for the furthering of scientific and medical understanding) or may be very practically orientated and of clear use to veterinary or medical science.

The pharmaceutical companies have to justify the expense of their research to their shareholders, so most of their research will be directed towards evaluating their existing products and developing new ones. To enter into this sort of work, it is important to have clearly thought through your stance on the ethics of animal experimentation. To some people it can never be justified; others believe that if the research results in the alleviation of human and animal disease, then some degree of animal suffering is acceptable. Obviously, if you are of the former persuasion, then this sort of work is not for you.

A related career option is the 'named vet'. In this job the vet's responsibility is to oversee the health and welfare of laboratory animals.

Ministry of Agriculture, Fisheries and Food
The Ministry of Agriculture, Fisheries and Food (MAFF) oversees the State Veterinary Services. Ministry vets are responsible for

testing for diseases such as tuberculosis and brucellosis, assisted by vets in private practice (Local Veterinary Inspectors, or LVIs). They enforce welfare regulations at markets and abattoirs, and ensure food safety for the public. They are also responsible for certification of animals for export, ensuring the details are correct and that they are fit enough to travel.

Also within the umbrella of MAFF are the Veterinary Investigation Centres, where vets diagnose disease by way of post mortem inspections and analysis of blood and tissue samples sent to them.

Ministry work is well paid, and there is little in the way of working unsociable hours. However, there is a lot of desk and paperwork involved, and there is little or no opportunity to treat sick animals.

Specialists

Further education and examinations are available to those who wish to specialise in smaller areas of the profession. Royal College approved certificates and diplomas exist in different subjects such as veterinary dermatology, cattle health and production and small animal medicine. To be able to call yourself a Specialist you must be approved as such by the Royal College, and positions are few and far between – only the creme de la creme need apply! However you can still see referrals, even without the title of Specialist, either in universities or private practice, in your own special interest subject, provided other vets recognise your expertise and are prepared to send their problem cases to you.

Lectureships and clinical teaching posts are also available in universities, which involve a combination of teaching vet students and seeing cases referred by other vets.

What qualifications and experience are needed?

In order to practice as a veterinary surgeon you must be a member of the Royal College of Veterinary Surgeons. Admission to the college is by a qualifying degree from one of the UK vet schools. These are:

● Bristol

● Cambridge

- Edinburgh

- Glasgow

- Liverpool

- London.

The courses offered for veterinary degrees are amongst the most oversubscribed of all university courses, with at least five people chasing every place. This is one of the reasons for the high A level grades required, as well as the academic demands of the course. But even if you are predicted, or already have, sufficiently high A level grades, this is not enough to guarantee you a place, because of the huge amount of competition. For this reason it is vital that you gain as many non-academic credits to put on your UCAS form as possible. These might include sporting achievements, school prefectships, hobbies and interests not necessarily animal related. Above all, though, it is vital to gain large amounts of appropriate work experience.

The minimum the vet schools ask for in A level grades at the present is two As and a B (or 28 points). It is unlikely you will get an offer if your predicted grades are lower than this. However, if you get an offer based on predicted grades, but then just miss the grades you were asked for, you may still be accepted if you are lucky. A clutch of high grade GCSEs helps if you have not yet taken A levels.

An alternate route is with a degree in a related subject, such as zoology, at 2:1 or higher. However, if you have already taken a degree you may have to fund the veterinary course yourself, and over five years this can be very expensive.

CASE STUDY

Alex Gough, veterinary surgeon, Sprinz & Nash veterinary hospital, Thame

I graduated from Cambridge vet school in 1996. I was academically well-prepared, but still had a lot to learn practically. I was thrown in at the deep end in a mainly farm animal practice in Wales. The first six months were constantly nerve-racking, but I soon learnt how to deal with all the common problems, and I had plenty of back-up from the older vets for the more complicated ones. One lasting memory is replacing a prolapsed womb into a cow at midnight, then the farmer's wife feeding me tea and cake in her nightie. Another is a horrendously difficult calving that took me three hours on the evening of the practice Christmas party.

After about a year I moved to a mixed, mainly small animal practice in Oxfordshire. This gave me plenty of opportunity to improve my small animal surgical skills, and make use of the advanced diagnostic equipment such as ECG monitors and blood biochemistry and haematology analysers. At the same time, there was still enough farm work to keep the job varied.

The contrast between the two practices, in different areas and the emphasis on different species, is marked. The on-call duties are a lot less onerous in the mainly small animal practice. I get called out less, and when I do get called out I usually see the animal in the surgery, rather than driving for half an hour there and half an hour back. On the other hand, it is harder to get to know the clients personally in a small animal practice, and I get less cake from farmers' wives.

It is over four years since I graduated and there are times, when it is busy or when cases don't progress as I would like, that I wonder if I should have made another career choice. But I enjoy what I do too much to ever change.

WORK EXPERIENCE

Figure 3 shows what work experience you should be aiming to get, from the age of 13 until you graduate.

Work experience whilst at school

Many teenagers work voluntarily with horses, and it can be difficult to find a placement. Look in *Yellow Pages* under Stables and Riding Schools, then ring around. Your work will primarily involve mucking out and feeding, but by being around horses and horse people you pick up the terminology, learn about management and learn to recognise what a healthy horse looks like.

You are required to get at least 12 weeks' work experience on farms from the age of 16 until your second or third year at university (depending which university), before you can proceed to the clinical stages of the course. You will need a signed certificate

Age	Establishment	Duties expected	Minimum amount
13–16	Vet practices Riding stables/ liveries	Observing, cleaning Mucking out, exercising and feeding horses	1–2 weeks/year Saturday/evening work or 1–2 weeks/ year
16–18	Vet practices	Observing, cleaning, possibly handling animals	Weekends/evenings or 2 weeks/year
	Farm work	Manual work, feeding, animal husbandry	Weekends/evenings or 2 weeks/year
Preclinical	Farm work	As above, plus dehorning, lambing, milking, general husbandry	12 weeks total
Early clinical years	Vet practices	Clinical examinations, administering medicines, performing diagnostic tests, observing	26 weeks in first 3 years
Final clinical year	Vet practices	As above, plus cat spays, bitch spays, minor surgery, assisting major surgery, rectal examination of cattle, foot trimming, lameness work ups in horses	26 weeks in last 3 years

Fig. 3.   What experience aspiring vets should get and when.

from each place you work at, giving the type of work, the address and the dates you were there. Leave a space for comments from the farmer – if they are complimentary to you, they can be helpful in getting a place at university or a job. You can make the certificates yourself, hand-written or on a computer. Alternatively, try writing to one of the vet schools, who often have their own blank certificates.

Again, use the *Yellow Pages* if you don't have any personal contacts with farmers. You should aim to get a week or two of work experience with each of pigs, sheep and cattle, both dairy and beef. This may not always be practical, depending on where you live, but it is essential to have spent at least some time on a farm, to convince the university admissions tutors that you are serious about the profession. This applies even if at the moment you think you will only work with dogs and cats, or horses, when you qualify. The universities are seeking all-rounders, who will only specialise at a later date.

The other essential is to gain as much time as possible working in veterinary practice. You can usually start this from 13 (but check with the practice first). It can be beneficial at this stage to spend most of your time in one practice. In this way you develop a rapport with the vets and nurses, and are likely to be allowed to do more. Most positions are unpaid, but some practices take on 'schoolies' to help with the general cleaning and day-to-day tasks in the evenings and Saturdays. Ring up or write – it doesn't hurt. Prepare for rejection though – these places are highly prized.

Many practices will only permit you to observe. Others, though, will get you to clean kennels and surgical instruments, restock drug shelves and sometimes hold animals for injections or tablets to be administered. Offer to help, it will always be appreciated even if there is nothing for you to do. And if you are given a job to do, do it. It looks terrible if you can't complete the tasks you are given. If you are not sure what you are supposed to be doing, ask. Also, bear in mind that your references at this stage will often be written by the nurses – the vets are usually too busy – so be nice to them!

After entering university

If you are lucky enough to get a place in a vet school you will have further work experience to do. As mentioned before you will need to get farm experience – 12 weeks minimum before entering your clinical years. The more, and the more varied, your experience, the better. At this stage there is no obligation to spend time working in veterinary surgeries, but it is useful to keep in touch with your local practice, even if it is only to pop in for a cup of tea. The preclinical years are often very academic, although the practical component is improving. But you may have forgotten what an animal looks like, come your summer holidays! Visiting your local practice will help remind you why you are doing all that hard work. Also, the vets may help you with your homework. Don't be too hopeful, though. The basic sciences such as biochemistry aren't that relevant to day-to-day general practice, and most vets forget the details soon after they graduate.

The clinical years

In the last three years of the university course you are expected to gain 26 weeks of work experience with vets ('seeing practice' or 'extramural studies') during your holidays. This should be with a variety of types of practices, such as horse specialists, farm practices and small animal practices. Some universities will require you to have a 'foster practice', where the majority of your seeing practice is spent. Even if this isn't a requirement, it is useful to build up a relationship with one practice. At this stage of your studies you are allowed to perform surgery and various other tasks, under a vet's supervision, and the more trust you have built up the more you will be allowed to do.

There is a pitiful grant available for seeing practice, approximately £3 per day, so don't blow all your student loan during term-time!

THE VETERINARY COURSE

The course to obtain a veterinary degree is five years long. The exception is Cambridge where it is six years and in your third year you study for a BA (later upgraded automatically to a MA); this can be in a related subject such as zoology, or something completely unrelated such as history of art.

The structure of the course varies from university to university, but generally the first two years (or three at Cambridge) are referred to as the preclinical years. Subjects covered in the preclinical years include:

- biochemistry

- physiology

- pharmacology

- nutrition

- animal husbandry

- pathology.

In the clinical years you will be taught the subjects relevant to modern veterinary work, including:

- cardiology

- dermatology

- soft tissue surgery

- orthopaedics

- horse, cattle and small animal medicine

- meat hygiene

- reproduction and obstetrics.

Job prospects

For the last 20 or so years, unemployment in the veterinary profession has been extremely low, as the numbers entering university are strictly controlled. However, in recent years the number of vets coming out of university has been too low, necessitating the employment of many vets from the continent and the Commonwealth. Consequently the number of students taken on has been increased, and they are just starting to come through the system now, making the job market more competitive than it has been for a while.

On the other hand, a high percentage of new graduates are female, and as some inevitably drop out of the profession to have families, even if only temporarily, it is unlikely that there will be any significant unemployment in the veterinary profession for some years to come.

At present the average starting salary is approximately £15,000 pa, with accommodation and car. This will vary from area to area and practice to practice.

AM I SUITED TO THE VETERINARY PROFESSION?

If you are considering this career, you should ask yourself the following questions:

- Am I academically able? High grades are needed at school, and lots of study is necessary to qualify.

- Do I enjoy working with animals?

- Do I enjoy working with people? The vet spends as much time with people as with animals, reassuring, advising and comforting. Interpersonal skills are very important.

- Am I physically fit? You will need to be physically fit to work with horses and farm animals, although this doesn't necessarily mean physically strong. In small animal work the physical side is less important, but certain disabilities may limit your ability to handle animals and perform surgery. If in doubt, contact one of the vet schools, or the Royal College of Veterinary Surgeons.

- Am I hard-working? Studying for A levels and then your degree is time-consuming and requires dedication. Furthermore, the job itself is tiring and stressful, often busy, and 60-hour weeks are not uncommon.

If you answered yes to all the above questions, then the veterinary profession may be for you. If not, then think carefully before continuing to aim for this rewarding but demanding profession.

VETERINARY NURSE

Job description
The modern veterinary nurse, or VN, is not merely an assistant to the veterinary surgeon, but a qualified professional in his or her own right. The Americans do not use the term veterinary nurse, but veterinary technician. The true VN, however, combines both descriptions. Certainly nursing is a large part of the job, and as with nurses of humans this includes:

- feeding

- bathing

- administration of medicines

- monitoring of vital parameters such as pulse, temperature and respiration rate.

Restraint of animals is a learned skill. They must be held safely but firmly, so no injury is caused to the animal, the nurse or the vet, and so the vet can carry out his or her examination or procedure.

Another important part of the veterinary nursing job is to monitor anaesthesia. Again, this is a skilled job. If the depth of anaesthesia during a surgical procedure is too light the animal may move, inconveniencing the surgeon and endangering the patient. It may even feel pain. On the other hand, if the level of anaesthesia is too deep, the animal may stop breathing and die.

The nurse monitors such parameters as gum colour, heart rate, respiration rate, presence of reflexes and eye position. In addition, some practices have complex anaesthetic equipment which takes measurements such as blood oxygen and blood pressure. Heart and respiratory monitors may also be used.

Legally, only a veterinary surgeon may make a diagnosis of a disease in an animal. However, the VN will assist in making that diagnosis by carrying out certain diagnostic procedures at the vet's direction. These include:

- taking and analysing blood samples

- collecting and analysing urine and faeces samples

- taking x-rays

- monitoring eating, drinking and other vital parameters

- recording electrocardiograms (ECGs).

Carrying out surgical procedures

Nurses are the only people, apart from vets and certain Home Office-licensed researchers, who may carry out surgical procedures in animals. The law at present allows qualified veterinary nurses to perform minor surgical procedures under the supervision of a vet, that 'do not enter a body cavity.' The precise definition of a body cavity is disputed, so while it is agreed that nurses should not be operating in the abdominal cavity, eg to spay a bitch, the Royal College has recently dictated that nurses should no longer perform castrations in cats, as this involves entering the scrotal sac. This has angered many vets and nurses, as in a number of practices nurses have been routinely castrating cats for many years. In theory it may be supposed that nurses should not enter the oral cavity (or mouth), but in practice nurses will often perform a lot of dental work. This involves scaling and polishing teeth and even performing extractions.

Other surgical procedures that nurses may be called upon to do include:

● removal of skin tumours

● stitching up of wounds

● draining aural haematomas (blood-filled swellings of the ear)

● amputation of tail tips or dew claws

● sterile assistance of a vet during major operations.

Whether you are allowed to do these things is at the discretion of the vet you work for.

Carrying out other procedures

Treatment of sick animals is under the direction of the vet, but you will often have to give the treatment yourself. This may be in the form of:

● tablets (and there is an art to getting them down an aggressive cat)

● injection (which may be under the skin, into the muscle or into the vein)

● fluids given by intravenous catheter

● bandaging and application of splints and casts.

There is also a fair amount of menial work. It is important that veterinary practices are kept clean and tidy, and the responsibility for this usually lies with the nurses. The nurses will also be responsible for cleaning and sterilising of surgical instruments.

Some practices will require veterinary nurses to live on the premises, often in a flat above the practice, at least while they are on duty. The duty rota depends on the number of nurses in the practice, but may be one evening and weekend in three or four. When on duty the nurse is responsible for checking, feeding and cleaning the in-patients, and alerting the duty vet if there are any problems. He or she also needs to be available in case the duty vet needs assistance, for example to perform anaesthesia for an emergency caesarean section on a bitch.

Most veterinary nurses spend the majority of their time working with small animals, even if they work in a mixed practice. Sometimes, though, they will be called upon to assist with operations on sheep and cattle, such as caesarean sections, or may be asked to help record details in large herd tuberculosis or blood tests.

Veterinary nurses are often employed in specialist equine practices, but here their role is usually different from that of their small animal counterparts. Because of the high value of some horses, and the relatively higher risks of anaesthesia, the anaesthetic is usually monitored by a vet, and sometimes more than one vet will operate on a horse at the same time. The responsibilities of the veterinary nurse in the equine surgical theatre are thus often limited to passing instruments and drugs, cleaning and sterilising.

Similarly, on the medical side, most of the diagnostic procedures such as x-rays and blood tests are carried out by vets. The legal exemption allowing qualified VNs to perform minor surgery applies only to pets, not to horses. Nurses will be responsible for mucking out stables, exercising the patients, and monitoring basic parameters such as urination, defecation, temperature and pulse.

Some practices aren't interested in veterinary nursing qualifications and place more emphasis on experience of working with horses and such qualifications as the BHS AI in stable management (see Chapter 4). Some practices do allow nurses to do more however, and there is a Royal College Certificate of Equine Nursing for those qualified nurses wishing to show their interest and expertise in this area.

What qualifications and experience are needed?

Legally, no qualifications are required to assist a veterinary surgeon. In fact there are many unqualified lay staff who help in veterinary practices, cleaning, looking after animals, even monitoring anaesthesia. However, only qualified veterinary nurses registered on the Royal College List of Nurses (ie ones who have paid their annual retention fee), are allowed to perform the minor surgical and medical procedures detailed above.

In order to begin training as a veterinary nurse it is necessary to have five GCSEs of grade C and above, including English or maths, and science. If you don't have these grades an alternative to retaking is to take the Pre-Veterinary Nursing course, a one-year examined qualification, passing which permits enrolment as a student nurse.

There is always competition for positions for trainee nurses. Often preference will be given to applicants who are personally known to the practice, so it can be an advantage to gain work experience with different local practices. Even if a position doesn't arise in that practice, the experience will be useful when applying for a job elsewhere, and you may be able to get a reference from the vets or nurses with whom you have worked.

It is important to make the most of your work experience. The same general rules for gaining experience applies for nurses as for vets. The important points are to be punctual, well-presented, cheerful and interested. This will make you a pleasure to work with, and you are more likely to be offered a job or get a good reference.

CASE STUDY

Naomi Sansom VN, Veterinary Nurse, Crossroads Veterinary Centre, High Wycombe

Naomi left school at 16 to work with horses. After getting her BHS AI in stable management, she decided to begin training as a veterinary nurse in order to further her horse career.

She joined a small animal practice in Teddington as a trainee, and passed both parts of her veterinary nursing examinations at the first attempt after a lot of hard work. At this stage she decided it was time to move on, away from home. However, at that time she found that most equine practices weren't interested in her nursing qualifications, so she took a job in a mixed (small animal, equine and farm animal) practice in Sussex. After she had been there approximately one year she became head nurse. She found, though, that the tasks of preparing the duty rota, ordering drugs, organising cover when people were sick, and supervising the nurses and the vets took time away from nursing duties.

One enduring memory was assisting the vet on a Sunday afternoon to save a young dog that was bleeding to death after being injured by a thrown stick. The grateful clients donated £200 to the practice! Another was helping in a caesarean section on an Irish wolfhound which had already had nine puppies, but had run out of energy to push out the last one.

At this practice she met her fiancé, a vet student. When he graduated she moved with him to Wales, but in that area there was no demand for qualified VNs. After nearly a year they moved to Buckinghamshire, and she now works 30 hours a week in a small animal practice. Fortunately she doesn't have to do any on-call work, so the job suits her well.

VETERINARY NURSE TRAINING

The majority of veterinary nurses complete their training while working in a veterinary practice. The practice must be a Royal College Approved Training and Assessment Centre (ATAC), also known as a Veterinary Nurse Training Centre (VNTC). The theoretical part of the course, together with some practical training, is undertaken at a number of different further education colleges and agriculture colleges, such as Berkshire College of Agriculture.

The course takes two years to complete, and can be undertaken on a day release or block release basis. There are examinations at the end of each year, and it is necessary to pass the first year exams (Part I), before progressing on to the final exams (Part II). Exams consist of written papers and practical/oral exams. Hard work and dedication are required – these are harder than GCSEs, and up to 50 per cent of candidates fail. You are allowed three attempts at each exam.

An alternative route to qualification as a veterinary nurse is to take a veterinary nursing degree. The first honours degree in veterinary nursing was approved in 1998. Universities currently offering veterinary nursing degrees include Bristol and Middlesex (see Appendix 1). The degree includes the Veterinary Nursing Certificate and S/NVQs.

Further exams can be taken after qualification. These include the Diploma in Advanced Veterinary Nursing (Surgical), and two new examinations, the Diploma in Advanced Veterinary Nursing (Medical) and the Certificate in Equine Nursing. You need to have at least two years experience as a qualified nurse in the relevant field to enrol.

Job prospects

As with those who want to be vets, it can be hard for aspiring veterinary nurses to get their feet on the first rung of the ladder. Getting the correct GCSEs and lots of work experience will help.

Once you are qualified, things look somewhat rosier. There is currently a high demand for qualified veterinary nurses, and since there is a relatively high drop-out rate from the mainly female profession for various reasons (eg pregnancy, disillusionment with unsociable hours), this situation will probably continue.

Trainee veterinary nurses can be quite poorly paid, often just the minimum wage. The salary for qualified nurses varies with location and experience, but starts from about £8,000. Accommodation may be provided, but this may only be a room in a flat above the practice.

AM I SUITED TO THE VETERINARY NURSING PROFESSION?

If you are considering this career, you should ask yourself the following questions:

● Do I enjoy caring for animals?

● Do I enjoy working with people? Nurses' duties include answering phones, advising and comforting clients, and reception work.

● Am I conscientious? The in-patients rely completely on the nurses for food, water, cleaning, medication and general care. If you are less than conscientious, the animals will suffer.

● Am I capable of the academic requirements? If you find it difficult to achieve the grades or pass the exams, you may struggle to qualify. But persistence and hard work often pay off.

● Do I have any health problems? Allergies to any species of domestic animal, phobias about certain species (eg rats), or physical problems such as a bad back, may make the nursing profession unsuitable for you.

● Am I squeamish? Some of the things you see in a veterinary practice may be unpleasant or distressing. Doing work experience at a vet's is the best way of discovering whether, for example, you can't stand the sight of blood.

● Can I put up with long hours and poor pay? The veterinary nursing profession doesn't necessarily offer you the best salary or the shortest hours that you can achieve. But most nurses who stay in the profession are doing it for the love of the job and the animals in their care.

USEFUL ADDRESSES AND WEB SITES

Veterinary and nursing colleges
Berkshire College of Agriculture, Hall Place, Burchetts Green, Maidenhead, Berkshire SL6 6QR. Tel: (01628) 824444.
Royal College of Veterinary Surgeons, Belgravia House, 62–64 Horseferry Road, London SW1P 2AF. Tel: (020) 7222 2001. www.rcvs.org.uk
University of Bristol, Department of Veterinary Medicine, Langford House, Langford, Bristol BS18 7DU. Tel: (0117) 928 9280.
University of Cambridge, Department of Clinical Veterinary Medicine, Madingley Road, Cambridge CB3 0ES. Tel: (01223) 337600.
University of Edinburgh, Royal (Dick) School of Veterinary Studies, Summerhall, Edinburgh EH9 1QH. Tel: (0131) 650 1000.
University of Glasgow, Veterinary School, 464 Bearsden Road, Bearsden, Glasgow G61 1QH. Tel: (0141) 339 8855.
University of Liverpool, Faculty of Veterinary Science, Liverpool L69 3BX. Tel: (0151) 794 4281.

Veterinary associations
British Small Animal Veterinary Association, Kingsley House, Church Lane, Shurdingham, Cheltenham, Gloucestershire GL51 5TQ. Tel: (01242) 862994. www.bsava.ac.uk

British Veterinary Association, 7 Mansfield Road, London W1M
0AT. Tel: (020) 7636 6541. www.bva.co.uk   bvahq@bva.co.uk
British Veterinary Nursing Association, The Seedbed Centre,
Coldharbour Road, Hawlow, Essex CM19 5AF. Tel: (01279)
450567. www.vetweb.co.uk/sites/bvna/index.htm

Government organisations

Meat Hygiene Service, Fosse House, 1–2 Peaseholme Green, York
YO1 2PX. Tel: (01904) 455501.
Ministry of Agriculture, Fisheries and Food, East Block, 10
Whitehall Place, London SW1A 2HH.

FURTHER READING

Getting into Veterinary Science, John Handley (Trotman).
Veterinary Nursing, Barbara Cooper VN Cert Ed, and Denis
Richard Lane BSc (Butterworth-Heinemann).

3

Working as a Paraprofessional

WHAT IS A PARAPROFESSIONAL?

A paraprofessional literally is someone who works alongside a professional. Specifically, in veterinary circles, a paraprofessional is thought of as a non-veterinary surgeon who provides some skilled aspect of animal healthcare. The term is usually used to refer to professions that work in the sphere of agriculture, such as bovine foot trimmers, artificial inseminators and ultrasound scanners. The definition could be more widely applied though, to include those working with companion animals and horses, for example farriers, equine dentists, pet behaviour counsellors and animal physiotherapists.

BOVINE FOOT TRIMMER

Job description

Cows spend most of their days on their feet, in conditions that vary from dry pasture to knee-deep slurry. They weigh approximately half a ton, so it is not surprising that they often develop foot problems.

Cows have two weight-bearing toes on each foot, and the cow's weight is distributed around the outside of each toe, so a footprint looks like a horseshoe. Foot problems come in a variety of shapes and forms, from infectious diseases such as foul in the foot or digital dermatitis, to inherited problems in foot conformation, to overgrown feet. Some of these problems need to be addressed by a veterinary surgeon, particularly the infectious diseases. However, the foot trimmer's job is to restore an overgrown or abnormal foot to its normal shape. By ensuring the cow evenly distributes her weight, the foot trimmer can not only cure lameness, but prevent lameness from recurring.

Many farmers take courses in foot trimming, or are taught by other farmers. The mobile specialist foot trimmer, however, can offer the farmer several advantages over DIY foot trimming:

- Higher levels of skill and experience.

- Labour paid for only when needed (these days farm labour is being cut back and spare hands are scarce).

- Special facilities, eg specialised foot trimming equipment, mobile foot trimming crush (cattle handling cage).

The work is physically demanding, and puts a lot of pressure on the back – a farmer may want you to trim 60 cows in a day. It is all year round work, but cattle suffer more foot problems in the winter when they are housed, so a lot of work will be done in cold weather.

What training and experience are needed?

No qualification is required by law to work as a foot trimmer, but obviously training is desirable. Courses are run by agricultural colleges. Alternatively, a longer apprenticeship can be undertaken. It is important to be experienced at handling bovines, and to understand their care and husbandry before setting up as a foot trimmer. This will enable you to more fully advise the farmer on prevention of foot problems, and avoid the situation of losing client confidence by lacking knowledge of the basics of their business.

A significant financial investment is also necessary. This involves foot trimming equipment such as rasps and hoof clippers as a minimum. Also important is a mobile crush, so you can visit small farms that do not have good handling facilities.

Job prospects

The future of the British agriculture industry is at present uncertain, with falling prices and the knock-on effect of loss of markets after the BSE crisis. Farmers are cutting back their expenses in all fields, and many prefer to tend their cows' feet themselves. However, cattle lameness does significantly affect production, so if the foot trimmer can persuade them it is in their interest to employ them, work may be found.

ARTIFICIAL INSEMINATOR

Job description

The traditional way of ensuring a constant supply of calves and milk from the farm's cows was to keep one or more bulls on the premises. These were allowed to run with the cows and fertilise them as they came into heat. This method is still widespread, but has significant disadvantages compared to the modern method of fertilisation – artificial insemination.

In this method, large fertility companies buy and keep prize bulls which have been proved to produce high-quality offspring with such characteristics as improved milk yield, ease of calving and good quality calves. The advantages of this method over keeping a bull are many. The farmer is spared the cost and trouble of buying and keeping a bull (and dairy bulls such as Friesians and Jerseys can be highly dangerous animals). With the artificial insemination method, he or she can choose the quality of bull to suit his or her pocket. A cheap tube or 'straw' of semen may be sufficient to get a cow in calf so she will continue to produce milk, a much more expensive one may be required if the offspring are to be kept to improve the genetic quality of the herd.

Some farmers go on courses themselves to learn how to implant the semen into the recipient cow. It is a skilled job, however, and most ask the fertility companies who sell the semen, such as Genus and Semex, to implant it. The fertility companies train and employ artificial inseminators. The job of the artificial inseminator is to travel from farm to farm with straws of frozen semen to inseminate the cows that the farmer selects. It is a skilled process – the straw must be threaded through the cow's cervix into the womb before releasing the sperm. If it is placed incorrectly, not only will the farmer have wasted the cost of the semen, but will also have to suffer the expense of his or her cow failing to conceive. Further, damage can be done to the cow by incorrect or over-forceful placement of the straw.

What training and experience are needed?

General experience handling and working with cattle is useful. Training is undertaken on cows' reproductive tracts that have been retrieved from abattoirs.

Job prospects

Although British livestock farming is going through a hard time at present, the field of artificial insemination is one area where farmers can't afford to cut back. Unless they go to the expense and inconvenience of maintaining a breeding bull, they will need artificial inseminators to provide the supply of calves and milk that their livelihood depends on. Whether more farmers will train to inseminate their own cows is debatable, but given the disastrous effects on business of a run of cows failing to conceive, it is likely that many will prefer to entrust the job to the professionals.

FARRIER AND EQUINE DENTIST

These jobs are discussed in more detail in Chapter 4, but both could be described as paraprofessionals.

PET BEHAVIOUR COUNSELLOR

Job description

Twenty years ago the field of pet psychology was derided as being somewhat cranky and unnecessary. Things have changed greatly, and pet behaviour counsellors are now recognised as highly skilled and important professionals. The biggest reason for the euthanasia of young dogs is behavioural problems (see Figure 4), so pet behaviour counsellors can really be seen as saving animals' lives, as well as their owners' sanity!

Most pet behaviour counsellors are self-employed. Many prefer to accept referrals mainly or solely from veterinary surgeons, and since medical treatment is often necessary as an adjunct to behavioural therapy, they will often need to work closely with the referring vet.

Dogs	**Cats**
Aggression	Urine spraying
Chasing behaviours	Aggression
Separation anxiety	Compulsive behaviour, eg overgrooming
Phobias	Phobias
Hypersexuality	Underattachment
Overattachment	Overattachment
Compulsive behaviour, eg licking	Pica (depraved appetite)

Fig. 4. Some common behavioural disorders in dogs and cats.

The job consists of talking to the owners of animals with behavioural problems to obtain a case history, and observing the animal's behaviour to come to a diagnosis. It may be possible to do all this on the pet behaviour counsellor's own premises, but often it will be necessary to travel to the owner's home to see the behaviour exhibited in the animal's own environment. Sometimes abnormal behaviour is shown only when there is no one around to see, such as the destructiveness of separation anxiety, and sophisticated surveillance techniques such as video cameras may be necessary.

Once a diagnosis of the behavioural problem is made, the pet behaviour counsellor must recommend treatment. As mentioned above, this will sometimes involve medical treatment under the direction of a vet, but often this is only a small part of the process. More important is the behavioural therapy, which involves training (both of animal and owner!) to permanently alter the animal's problem behaviour. All households and situations are different, and it will often take some careful planning and lateral thinking to achieve the required results. It will also take patience. By the time an animal is referred to the pet behaviour counsellor the behavioural problem is usually severe and long-standing, and it can take a long time to remedy. A significant minority will fail to be cured, sometimes because of the nature of the problem, sometimes because of lack of owner compliance with the counsellor's instructions.

ANIMAL PHYSIOTHERAPIST

Job description
Physiotherapy involves the treatment of disease by physical methods rather than drugs or surgery. It is of particular importance in injuries of the musculoskeletal system – the bones, muscles, tendons and ligaments. These can become damaged in various ways, through exercise or trauma for example. Sometimes they will need surgery or medicines to help them heal, but physiotherapy is useful to speed recovery.

A quick recovery is obviously desirable in all cases, but it is of particular importance to get full function as soon as possible in athletic animals. Thus animal physiotherapists often spend a great deal of time with working and competing animals, such as police dogs, greyhounds and horses.

Techniques used in physiotherapy include massage and manipulation of joints and soft tissue, electrotherapy such as muscle stimulators, hydrotherapy including hot and cold baths and swimming, and advice on exercise regimes to encourage strengthening of muscles, tendons and ligaments.

Treatment is usually at the request of a veterinary surgeon, although the exact form that treatment takes is often left to the skill and judgement of the physiotherapist.

What qualifications and experience are needed?

Theoretically there is no legal requirement to be qualified before you can call yourself a physiotherapist. However, to call yourself a chartered physiotherapist you have to be able to demonstrate a high level of academic and practical training, which in practice means being a Member of the Chartered Society of Physiotherapy (MCSP).

To qualify as a Chartered Physiotherapist it is necessary to first complete a degree in physiotherapy, such as the BSc in physiotherapy. This is offered by many universities including

- Birmingham

- Bristol

- Cardiff

- Edinburgh

- Leeds

- Brunel (London)

- Manchester

- Nottingham

- Sheffield

- Ulster.

Once you have qualified in human physiotherapy, it is then necessary to undertake a further two years in general practice and attend courses in animal therapy that are certified by the Association of Chartered Physiotherapists in Animal Therapy (ACPAT). The ACPAT divides practising Chartered Physiotherapists into two categories. Category B members must work under the direct supervision of a veterinary surgeon, while Category A members can work independently, provided they have veterinary permission.

USEFUL ADDRESSES AND WEB SITES

Association of Pet Behaviour Consultants, PO Box 46, Worcester WR8 9YS. Tel: (01386) 751151. abpc@petbcent.demon.co.uk

De Montfort University Lincoln, Caythorpe Court, Caythorpe, Nr Gratham, Lincs NG32 3EP. (Offers BSc in Animal Science, Behavioural Studies.)

Rachel Casey MRCVS, Animal Behaviour Clinic, School of Science, Technology and Health, University of Southampton New College, The Avenue, Southampton SO17 1BG. (Information about certificate in Applied Animal Behaviour.)

The Secretary, The Association of Chartered Physiotherapists in Animal Therapy (ACPAT), Morland House, Salters Lane, Winchester SO22 5JP. (Enclose an sae.) acpat@clara.net .http://www.acpat.clara.net

The Chartered Society of Physiotherapy, 14 Bedford Row, London WC1R 4ED.

4

Working with Horses

JOBS WITH HORSES

To work with horses is the dream of many, so this is a competitive field, often with low pay, due to the number of youngsters prepared to help out for free. Any experience with horses will help your chances of finding a job. You can get experience working in livery yards, hunt stables, riding schools and specialist equine veterinary practices. Most people who want to work with horses will already be interested in riding. Having lessons in riding will help with your general competence with the species, including handling, getting used to working with tack and understanding horse terminology. This last is important – the horse world sometimes seems to speak its own language, and it is a language you will have to talk and understand to be accepted as a competent professional or employee.

It is worth noting that if you are considering a career associated with hunting, your future may not be assured. At the time of writing a bill is being discussed by Parliament to ban hunting live prey with dogs. Whether this bill succeeds or not, this is an issue that isn't likely to go away, with the majority of people in the country supporting a ban. If a ban does come into force there may be some reduction in the number of jobs in the hunting industry, although many people might find drag hunting an acceptable, animal welfare friendly alternative.

STABLE LAD/GROOM

Job description
The stable lad (called a lad whether male or female) or groom is responsible for the day-to-day care of the horses on a yard, such as a stud farm or livery stables. Daily tasks include:

- feeding

- watering

- mucking out

- exercising (lungeing, hacking, walking, schooling over jumps or just turning out)

- grooming

- cleaning tack

- taking hay and food deliveries

- cleaning out feet

- removing manure and poisonous plants such as ragwort from pasture.

Qualifications, experience and prospects

No qualifications are needed to start work as a stable lad or groom, but experience of riding and handling horses is important. This is usually obtained on a voluntary basis through school or personal contacts. It is also useful to be a competent rider, and to have had riding lessons and passed some of the BHS exams. Entrants to BHS exams must be at least 16 years old. There are four levels of examination, Stage 1 demonstrating a basic knowledge of horse care, while Stage 4 demonstrates the candidate is capable of taking charge of a group of horses without supervision. The Association of British Riding Schools has its own examination system, including a Groom's Certificate and Diploma.

Opportunities exist for work as a stable lad or groom in liveries, stud farms, riding schools and racing yards. Many people view a job as a stable lad as the first step on the ladder to another career with horses, giving the opportunity to become competent in horse handling and stable management, while also allowing time to ride and improve riding skills. A job as a stable lad may therefore lead on to a career as a jockey, show jumper or riding instructor.

Because of the obvious attractions of this job to those who enjoy riding and being with horses, and the lack of qualifications necessary to begin, it can be difficult to get a job and pay is usually poor. Until recently riding schools commonly took on 'working pupils', providing accommodation, food and training, but no pay in return for general work. More recently, however, the BHS has begun the BHS Apprenticeship Scheme. Although apprentices are exempt from the national minimum wage, the BHS standards ensure the apprentices aren't exploited, ie that they work no more than 40 hours per week, receive at least four hours of formal riding instruction per week, and receive a minimum hourly wage, currently about £1.40 for the youngest first year apprentices. However, some deductions may be made for food and accommodation.

STABLE MANAGER

Job description
There are several different sorts of stables, including:

- riding schools

- livery yards

- stud farms

- polo yards

- hunt stables

- racing yards.

They all require someone to be in charge of them, to look after the day-to-day running. The stable may be run by the owner or part-owner, or by a manager employed by the owner. To own or buy a stables obviously requires a very large investment in capital – an option open to very few. Stable management is a more attainable career for many, although the number of jobs available is not high.

Running a stables entails a wide range of responsibilities. As a stable manager you would be responsible for organising the staff to ensure all necessary tasks are carried out, dealing with employment difficulties, hiring and firing, buying in supplies of feed and bedding and organising pasture care. How much help you get in these tasks depends on the size of the stables and the number of horses and employees. If you run a small livery with half a dozen horses, you may end up doing most of the work yourself. If you run a major Newmarket racing yard, you will have many people working for you to whom you can delegate responsibility.

The different types of stables provide different challenges. For example, if you run a riding school you must ensure the quality of your teaching staff, the suitability of mounts (a skittish stallion is unsuitable for beginners), appropriate insurance and advertising of services. You will also be liable to a yearly inspection under the Riding Establishments Act. A livery yard manager must ensure that stables animals are vaccinated against equine influenza to prevent outbreaks of flu affecting other animals. The stud yard manager has this worry too, and also has to safeguard against venereally transmitted diseases such as contagious equine metritis. All stable managers need to be alert to signs of disease, ill health or injury, and seek appropriate help from professions as necessary.

What training and experience are needed?
The BHS examinations in stable management give a good grounding in running stables and caring for the horses in them. However, unless you are lucky enough to own or be able to buy a stables, it is likely that you will need considerable experience in horse management, and working upwards from a position such as stable lad will be the usual route of entry into this job. Working in a variety of horse-related jobs will broaden your experience, but it is important to have spent a reasonable length of time in just one job to demonstrate stability, reliability and responsibility.

FARRIER

Job description
A farrier, put simply, shoes horses. On the face of it this may seem a simple, if physically tough, profession. However, there is a great skill to farriery involving a deep understanding of the anatomy of the horse's limbs, and the uses to which horses are put, as well as

good knowledge of the diseases and abnormal conditions of the horse's foot. The job is skilled, and the potential for damage and suffering is so great if the work is performed badly, that only a properly qualified and registered farrier is allowed, under the Farriers (Registration) Act of 1975, to shoe a horse or work as a farrier. The Act defines farriery as 'any work in connection with the preparation or treatment of the feet of a horse for the immediate reception of a shoe thereon, the fitting by nail or otherwise of a shoe to the foot or the finishing of such work to the foot.'

Farriers also need to have skills as a blacksmith, in order to work the iron into the required shape for the foot. A blacksmith is simply someone who works with iron, but unless they are a registered farrier they cannot shoe horses.

The farrier is usually called by a client to shoe or remove the shoes of one or more horses. Horse shoes not only protect the feet from wear and tear on hard ground, but can be shaped to provide orthopaedic support. For example, by raising the heels of the shoe, stress can be taken off certain tendons, and a shoe with a strut across the middle (heart-bar shoe) provides support and relief for horses suffering with laminitis. Farriers often work closely with veterinary surgeons to treat horse lameness, and a good farrier is important to a horse's continued ability to work or compete. A poorly fitted shoe, however, can have disastrous consequences, such as lameness and the formation of abscesses.

When presented with a foot to shoe, the farrier first cleans the foot and looks for signs of ill health, then trims it to the ideal shape. He or she then measures and shapes a shoe and fixes it to the foot, usually by nails driven into the insensitive part of the hoof. This is then repeated with the other three feet. The work is physically demanding, and since the farriers spend most of their time bent over, back problems are common and often restrict the length of a farrier's career.

What qualifications and experience are needed?

To become a farrier it is necessary to serve an apprenticeship of four years and two months with an Approved Training Farrier (ATF) – a registered farrier with a fixed forge who has been approved to train apprentices by the Farriers Registration Council. Two months are classified as a probationary period, during which the ATF assesses the apprentice. During these two months, either the ATF or the apprentice can terminate the apprenticeship agreement. Twenty-one weeks of the training will be at an Approved Training Centre, currently offered by Warwickshire College, Herefordshire College of Technology and Oatridge Agricultural College in Edinburgh.

There are certain minimum requirements to begin as an apprentice farrier. Applicants must be 16 years or over and must have passed four GCSEs at grade C or above, including English language. Alternatively, it is possible to take an entrance examination if the applicant doesn't possess the required grades, or examinations of similar academic merit. The entrance examination is scheduled twice a year. It is one hour long, and consists of a written paper testing basic English, maths and graphical abilities. Applicants must also take a medical examination (at their own expense) including an eye test and a test for colour blindness. Colour blindness and learning difficulties do not necessarily preclude an applicant from acceptance, but allowance for these problems is at the discretion of the college.

Grants are available to help with the cost of training for applicants under the age of 25. If you are over 25 you will have to bear the cost of training yourself, currently approximately £6,500 for the four years and two months, including 21 weeks of college training. To become an apprentice it is necessary to be proposed by an ATF. The Farriery Training Service has a list of ATFs, available if you send a stamped addressed A4 envelope with two first class stamps.

CASE STUDY

Matt Pinney DWFC, farrier

Matt Pinney has been working as a qualified farrier for three-and-a-half years, since completing his four-year and two-months apprenticeship. He trained with a Master Farrier in the field, and also spent a total of 28 weeks through the four years of training at Hereford School of Farriery. This culminated in the DWCF qualification (Diploma of the Worshipful Company of Farriers).

Matt now specialises in polo pony shoeing (being a professional polo player himself as well). This means the summers are very busy. A typical day starts at 5.30 am, when he travels to the polo yard and begins work. Shoeing eight ponies is a good day's work, but it is not uncommon to be required to shoe ten to twelve, and then he feels it the next day! The day is made even more tiring, since he often plays polo in the late afternoon, and then may need to do further shoeing afterwards. From time to time he works an 18-hour day!

In the winter he is less busy since he is shoeing arena polo ponies only, and just needs to shoe their front feet. This leaves him time to break in youngsters of his own.

One enduring memory is his time spent in Kenya, teaching farriery to grooms who had no formal training, but were expected to shoe with very limited equipment and stock.

Matt finds it very rewarding performing corrective and surgical work on the chronically lame to give them a new lease of life when the situation looks hopeless. But he finds it hard working seven days a week for six months solid, often having to be available on nearly a 24-hour-call-out, and still offering a consistently high standard of service. He also dislikes bad-mannered horses that attempt to injure him with little restraint from the owners, and he feels that the public (and some vets) view farriers as archetypal blacksmiths with more brawn than brains, despite the extensive training.

That said, he would probably choose the same career again, although with hindsight he says he would probably have structured his life slightly better!

EQUINE DENTIST

Job description
Horses' teeth erupt continuously throughout their lives, wearing down as they chew grass and hay. Sometimes the teeth wear abnormally, leading to sharp spurs developing, which can lacerate their cheeks and tongue. The main job of the equine dentist is to keep the horse's teeth in good condition, by means of tooth rasps and other equipment. Some equine dentists perform extractions. This is a controversial area, and the matter has been discussed in Parliament, since some believe that tooth extraction is an act of veterinary surgery, and as such should only be carried out by veterinary surgeons. The situation is currently under review.

What qualifications and experience are needed?
Currently there is no requirement for a specific qualification or registration before beginning practice as an equine dentist, and although training courses are available it is a concern to many that

a certificate of proficiency in equine dentistry can be obtained after just three weeks. It is likely that, at some point in the near future, tighter rules regarding the practice of equine dentistry in the UK will be introduced.

In the mean time, expertise and experience handling horses is obviously necessary, since many will become quite skittish when their mouths are examined or their teeth rasped.

COMPETING WITH HORSES

There are a number of competitive sports involving horses which provide employment opportunities, including:

- flat racing

- National Hunt racing

- show jumping

- dressage

- polo

- eventing

- endurance riding.

These are discussed further below.

A large number of people are employed in the competitive equine industry, (about 35,000 in racing alone), both hands-on horse professionals such as farriers, grooms and trainers, as well as those dealing less directly with the horses themselves such as the clerk of the course (responsible for race course maintenance), stewards, tack makers and those involved in the betting industry.

A less predictable, but potentially more profitable way of making a living from the competitive equine arena, is to ride the competing horses. Top jockeys can earn high salaries, but for every jockey who makes it there are dozens who never achieve success.

To be a successful jockey you must be physically fit, light (hence most jockeys are short), a skilled and experienced rider, and also capable of getting the most from your mount. Jockeys are judged by results, and one that fails to win races will not command a high salary or a job for long.

It can be difficult to get started as a competing equestrian. For some the chance will come by working their way up from stable lad. Others may own one or more horses, and make a name for themselves at small races. It can help to be near one of the well-known centres for horse-riding, such as Newmarket. Here there is a large concentration of people associated with the equine world in general, and horse racing in particular, and consequently there will be more and better quality jobs and opportunities available.

There are no hard-and-fast rules guaranteed to make you a success in any competitive sport, but if you have natural ability, determination and the right opportunity, you have as much chance of success as anyone.

Flat racing

The first racecourse in England was set up in Chester during the reign of Henry VIII. Racing has taken place in Britain ever since, overseen by the Jockey Club which was set up in 1750. Races can be of three types: handicaps which give advantages to weaker horses by weighting the quicker ones; weight-for-age races, which weight down more experienced horses; and selling races, in which the winning horse is sold at auction at the end of the race.

There is no standard racecourse, and they are of different lengths and can be run left- or right-handed. On the day of the race the horses are fitted with lightweight racing shoes. Half-an-hour before the race they are paraded in the paddock. The jockeys then mount and they move down to the starting stalls. A white flag raised means they are all in and under starter's orders. The starter then presses a button to release the gates.

The judge watches at the finishing post, to declare the winner and two runners-up, using photographic evidence if necessary. Finally the jockeys are weighed to confirm they and their saddle are the correct weight.

S/NVQs are offered by the Racing and Thoroughbred Breeding Training Board (RTBTB) at three levels: Horse Care, Racehorse Care, and Racehorse Care and Management. The racing schools train stable staff, and the best riders get a chance to become apprentice jockeys. They remain apprentices until reaching the age of 25, or riding 95 winners.

National Hunt racing

Also known as steeplechasing, National Hunt racing involves jumping fences or hedges. The pace is slower than flat racing, but more skill is required on the part of the horse, and so the horses tend to compete for longer, up to eight years, unlike flat racers which usually retire after a couple of years.

The first Grand National was run in 1839 over natural obstacles, but later standard-sized fences were used. There are three types of fences: plain, open ditch and water jump. There is a minimum distance of two miles and the Grand National is the longest at 4 miles 865 yards. Horses that jump tend to be stouter in build than flat racers. They are often geldings, for reasons of temperament and to prevent damage when jumping, so there is little in the way of a breeding industry concerned with Hunt Racing.

An amateur version of the steeplechase is the point to point, originally run round posts marking out a temporary course, but now consisting of fences similar to a steeplechase. Riders are not paid, and prize money is low.

Show jumping

The first International Horse Show was held at Olympia in London in 1907, and show jumping was included in the 1912 Olympic Games. In the 1970s the British authorities set strict rules to define who was a professional, and now there is a year-round professional circuit, with the two major events in the UK being the Horse of the Year Show and the Royal International Horse Show.

There are a large number of different courses, involving high and spread fences and walls, Derby banks and water jumps. A set time is allowed in which to complete the course, and penalty points are given for exceeding the allotted time, knocking down a fence, falling or putting a foot in water.

Show jumping requires a lot of training and skill on the part of both rider and horse. There has been some decline in popularity in recent years, at least as a spectacle, and the BBC no longer televises the Horse of the Year Show.

Dressage

Like show jumping, dressage was first included in the Olympic Games in 1912. Unlike show jumping, however, which is marked objectively on faults, dressage is marked subjectively by judges on style. The judges award marks for regularity of paces, suppleness, eagerness and elasticity. The rider should be well-balanced, and his or her positioning of the horse needs to be exact.

Training horse and rider for dressage takes years and requires dedication and patience.

Eventing

Eventing is regarded by many as the ultimate test of horsemanship, comprising as it does different disciplines requiring pace, skill, fitness and versatility. The best known form of eventing is the three-day event, as exemplified by the Badminton Horse Trials. To compete in the three-day event horses must be at least five years old, and their riders at least 18 years old. Penalty points are awarded for faults, and the winner is the competitor at the end of the competition with the least number of points.

Day one is the dressage. Day two is the cross-country, which tests speed and endurance, and day three is the show jumping. Veterinary inspections at different stages ensure the horse is fit to continue.

The cross-country stage is possibly the most exciting, but demanding, part of the three-day event, requiring jumping ability, speed and stamina on the part of the horse, and endurance, knowledge of pace and judgement of the lie of the country on the part of the rider. It is also the most dangerous part of the three-day event, and in 1999 four people died at different cross-countries around Britain.

Hunting

While not technically a competitive sport, hunting is classed as a field sport, so merits inclusion here. There is a large industry involved in hunting in Britain, with many people employed in areas such as looking after and training the fox hounds and caring for the horses.

The season begins on 1st November, when less damage is likely to be done to crops. Dress is formal. Fox hunting is the most popular form of hunting, with over 200 fox-hound packs in Britain.

As mentioned at the beginning of the chapter, hunting is under threat, and choosing this way of life as a career may not provide much job security for the future.

Endurance riding

This is an upcoming sport, but at present most riders own and train their own horses and have full- or part-time jobs elsewhere to pay for the sport. However, there does seem to be an increase in interest in the sport currently, and the number of yards specifically training endurance horses may grow. At the moment there is no prize money for competitions.

Polo

Polo was invented in the Far East about 2,000 years ago, and adopted by the British when they ruled India. The ponies have to be quick and agile, able to stop, turn and gallop off in another direction without hesitation. The polo player must be capable of controlling his or her pony with one hand, and be able to lean to the sides.

The game is played on a field with goals at either end, and the length of the match is split into seven-minute chukkas. There are four to six chukkas in a game. Each team has four players and a goal is scored when the ball passes between the posts. A handicap system exists, so weaker teams are given a head start.

The game is physically demanding, so a pony is only allowed to play in two chukkas per match. Usually one pony is used per chukka, with a spare in case of injury.

CASE STUDY

James Neary, polo team player, manager and coach

After gaining three A levels James took up polo-playing professionally. He qualified as a Hurlingham Polo Association approved coach and as an umpire, and also took a first aid course. He has now been working in professional polo for two years, and currently brings in about £24,000 per year, with a house provided.

He starts the day by checking the horses, then gives the grooms the order of the day, such as whether the horses are playing, need schooling, normal exercise or a day off. He then phones his boss and lets him know what is happening.

Later in the day he spends time organising club games, and also phones other polo professionals to inform them of arrangements. Routine agricultural tasks are also important, such as paddock and pitch maintenance, and ensuring feed supplies are in good order and being obtained at a good price.

It is necessary to keep meticulous records on each horse, such as when it was last shod and wormed, and if it has been kicked, when and where, as well as other health and performance records. He also gives polo lessons to a range of ages and group sizes.

The job is high-pressure – James feels it is necessary to perform well for him to retain his position, and tries to remain professional at all times, both on and off the pitch. He would definitely choose the same career again, and considers his pay and career prospects good, but dislikes the long working hours and the cut-throat nature of the sport.

USEFUL ADDRESSES AND WEB SITES

Animal Care and Equine Training Organisation (ACETO), Second Floor, The Burgess Building, The Green, Stafford ST17 4BL. www.aceto.co.uk

The Association of British Riding Schools, Queens Chambers, 38–40 Queen Street, Penzance, Cornwall TR18 4BH.

British Dressage, Stoneleigh Park, Kenilworth, Warwickshire. www.britishdressage.co.uk

The British Horse Society, Training Office, Stoneleigh Park, Kenilworth, Warwickshire CV8 2LR. Tel: (01203) 696697. www.bhs.org.uk

The British Racing School, Snailwell Road, Newmarket, Suffolk CB8 7NU.

The Farrier Training Service, Sefton House, Adam Court, Newark Road, Peterborough PE1 5PP. Tel: (01733) 319770. frc@farrier-reg.demon.co.uk

Herefordshire College of Technology, Folly Lane, Hereford HR1 1LS.

The Jockey Club, 42 Portman Square, London W1H 0EN. www.thejockeyclub.co.uk/thejockeyclub info@thejockeyclub.co.uk

Mick Easterby Racing, www.mickeasterby-racing.co.uk (A trainer's web site.)

Oatridge Agricultural College, Ecclesmachan, Broxburn, West Lothian EH52 6NH.

Polonet UK, www.polonet.co.uk (Polo links.)

Warwickshire College, Royal Leamington Spa and Moreton Morrell, Moreton Morrell, Warwick CV35 9BL.

FURTHER READING

The Horse, A complete encyclopaedia, Pam Cary *et al.* (Ivy Leaf).
The Manual of Horsemanship (Threshold Books Ltd).
Veterinary Notes for Horse Owners, H Hayes (Stanley Paul).

5

Working with Dogs and Cats

JOBS WITH DOGS AND CATS

There is a wide variety of jobs involving dogs and cats (some of which are dealt with in other chapters). The pet care industry in the UK is large and often profitable, bearing out the old saying that Britain is a nation of animal lovers (and also the one that where there's muck there's brass!). In general, people are prepared to spend money on their pets because of the close emotional bond they have with them. This money may be spent on essentials such as food and veterinary care, or non-essentials which are for the pleasure of the owner or animal, such as toys, comfortable beds and decorative collars.

This close attachment that owners have to their pets, however, brings a responsibility to those whose duty it is to care for the animals. Many owners regard their pets as members of the family, and demand as much patience, attention to detail and quality of service as they would for themselves or their children.

KENNEL HAND

Job description
Dogs and cats rely heavily on humans for food, shelter and social interaction. These are provided on a day-to-day basis by their owners, but often situations arise where, for a limited time, the owner is unable to do this. There are various possible reasons, including:

- holidays

- illness or stays in hospital

- moving house or decorating

- business trips

- having visitors to stay who are allergic to or don't like pets.

People will often ask a friend to look after a pet in times of need, but this is not always practical. In these cases the answer is to put the pet into a boarding kennel or cattery. Some establishments specialise in dogs or cats, some take both, but they all provide a secure environment for the animals in warm, comfortable, escape-proof accommodation, and all provide food, water and cleaning.

Standards of boarding establishments vary greatly. The best will have areas for the pets to exercise, enclosed areas with safe heaters, comfortable bedding, regular cleaning out and feeding, and policies on vaccination to prevent the spread of communicable diseases. Unfortunately, some places fall short of these standards.

Jobs in boarding kennels and catteries are essentially similar. A boarding establishment worker or owner is responsible for admitting animals, taking all their details such as name, preferred diet, known medical conditions, details of any medication required, vaccination status and length of stay.

Once the animals have been admitted and placed in their own runs, they will need periodic checking to make sure they are settling in okay. In a typical day the kennel worker lets the animals out for exercise into a secure run, cleans out the kennel, lets them back in and provides them with fresh food and water. This is repeated for all the boarders at various intervals throughout the day. The animals must also be monitored regularly for signs of ill health, such as vomiting, diarrhoea or general lethargy, and veterinary treatment sought if necessary.

What qualifications and experience are needed?
Little is needed in the way of qualifications and experience to work in boarding kennels. However, certain attributes are desirable, and will help you get a job and be more competent when you start working. Experience working with dogs and/or cats is useful, either as a work experience student in a kennels, or in a different job working with these species. Also, if you own a dog

or cat you will have a better understanding of what these animals need. You should be confident handling them, and be able to give tablets and sometimes, for example with diabetic patients, injections.

Two qualifications that demonstrate competence working with dogs and cats are the Certificate of Small Animal Care, available at Further Education Colleges, and the Pre-Veterinary Nursing Examination, which is taken from within a veterinary practice. This latter qualification is intended for those who want to enter the veterinary nursing profession, but if for any reason you decide not to progress on to the VN examinations and leave the profession, the pre-vet nursing exam is a good grounding and evidence of competence in small animal care.

QUARANTINE KENNEL WORKER

Quarantine was introduced to protect the UK from diseases transmitted by mammals that are prevalent in other countries, notably rabies. Until 1999 any dog or cat entering the country from any other country outside the British Isles has been required to stay in quarantine kennels for a period of six months. If, after this time, it has shown no signs of disease, it is allowed into the country.

The quarantine rules are currently changing, and in February 2000 the Pet Travel Scheme was introduced, allowing fully vaccinated animals from certain countries to come into the UK without the need for quarantine. However, animals without the correct certification or vaccinations, or from non-approved countries, will still need to spend six months in quarantine. There will thus be a need for quarantine kennels for the foreseeable future.

The job of working in a quarantine kennels is essentially the same as for a boarding kennels. There are some important differences, however. It is vital for all the workers to monitor the boarders for signs of ill health, and seek appropriate veterinary advice if necessary. It is sensible for quarantine kennel workers to be vaccinated against rabies, since it is possible they will come into contact with rabies carriers.

DOG GROOMER

Job description

Certain breeds of dog, such as Afghan hounds and bearded collies, have long hair. Their coats rapidly become unkempt, dirty and knotted if they aren't combed regularly. But even with regular attention from the owner the coats can become untidy, and in the worst, neglected cases, become dirty and smelly, trapping urine and faeces, which leads to damage to and infection of the skin. A thick, matted coat is also a haven for parasites such as fleas.

Many pet owners make regular appointments with groomers to prevent the coats getting to this stage. The benefits of regular grooming include:

● improved aesthetic appearance

● healthier skin and coat

● reduction of 'doggy' smell.

Dog groomers will also often pick up signs of ill health related to the skin such as parasite infestation, skin infections and abnormal lumps and bumps, and can advise owners when veterinary attention should be sought.

A further need for dog grooming arises from the show circuit, for which dogs must be clipped and groomed to stringent and specific standards set out by the Kennel Club. A good groomer is invaluable to the person involved in showing, to help them gain good results in the show ring.

Some groomers have their own premises, and ask that dogs are brought to them. Others offer a mobile service, visiting the owner's home. Grooming salons may also be found in pet shops, garden centres and boarding or breeding kennels.

Sometimes weekend work will be necessary to enable the service to be offered to those in full-time work.

The work includes:

● bathing, shampooing and drying

● clipping and trimming

● nail-clipping

● teeth-cleaning

● ear-cleaning

● treatment for parasites.

What training and experience are needed?

To enter a career as a dog groomer you should be confident with dogs and able to handle them firmly but gently. Bear in mind that dogs can be nervous, aggressive, or over-friendly, all of which make the job more difficult. You will need patience with the animal, a friendly manner with the client, good hand-eye co-ordination and an eye for good artistic or aesthetic effect.

There are three ways of gaining sufficient experience and qualifications to work as a groomer. One is to gain skills on the job with training by an appropriately qualified groomer. The second is, for those between 16 and 17 years, a place on a Youth Training Programme. Thirdly there are private courses at grooming training centres, for which a fee must be paid.

Once you have 18 months of experience as a dog groomer you can enrol for the City and Guilds Dog Grooming Certificate 775. This is a two-part exam, with a written and a practical component, which demonstrates your competence in grooming. There is also an Advanced Grooming Diploma, which requires a detailed knowledge of Kennel Club Breed Standards, styles and trimming techniques. This consists of a written paper and seven practical modules, and demonstrates a sufficiently advanced level of skill to groom animals for the show ring.

CASE STUDY

Robert Lyons, dog and cat groomer

Robert has been grooming dogs and cats for 30 years, and for this job he considers practice and experience as important as academic qualifications. The day is spent collecting the animals, then washing, grooming and drying them. Some will need trimming, either because of mats or to achieve the recognised breed-standard cut. He then returns the animals home. Other regular tasks he performs include trimming nails and checking teeth, anal glands and skin.

His most memorable experience is doing well in the Dog Groomer of the Year competition, and he finds it rewarding turning a shaggy, matted animal into a smart, clean and comfortable one. However, some cases he has seen have been so matted, he considers them to have been cruelly neglected. He would choose the same career again, but finds the career prospects, working hours and status in the public eye disappointing.

DOG WARDEN

Job description
Contrary to the popular image of dog wardens, the job is essentially altruistic, involving reuniting lost dogs with their owners, and taking strays off the streets where they cause a nuisance and a hazard to traffic and themselves.

It is a law under the 1992 Environmental Protection Act for all local authorities to employ an officer who is responsible for the collection of strays. The job involves responding to calls and complaints from the public, which may concern barking, scavenging, fouling and other problems. Dog wardens may be involved with owned dogs that cause a nuisance, particularly those that are allowed to wander the streets. Many local authorities have areas designated as no fouling, and areas where dogs must be kept on leads, and dog wardens help police these areas.

Dog wardens also have a role in promoting responsible dog ownership, encouraging owners to clear up when their dog fouls, keep them under control in public places and generally act with consideration for others.

What qualifications and experience are needed?
No specific qualifications are necessary except a full driving licence, although numeracy and literacy are an advantage. It is useful to have experience working with and handling dogs, but it is also important to have good interpersonal skills. Unlike many other jobs working with animals, a lot of the interactions with people will be confrontational, with the public often being unappreciative of the dog warden's work.

On the job training is usually provided, and further training comes in the form of periodic seminars and lectures.

DOG TRAINER

Job Description
Dog trainers are in demand in a number of fields, so dogs can be trained to serve a number of purposes. These include:

- obedience training for pet dogs

- agility training for competing dogs

- sheepdog and gundog training for working dogs

- guide dog and other assistance dog training

- training for Customs and Excise 'sniffer' dogs

- training for Service dogs such as attack/patrol dogs, search and rescue dogs

- guard dog training for private security firms.

There are a number of different training methods, from the physical punishment-based methods, to those based purely on rewards. Most trainers use a mix of reward and punishment, although punishment does not have to be painful such as beatings, but can be water pistols, loud noises or withholding of rewards such as treats or attention.

Training Service dogs and guide dogs are specialist jobs, and more details are given in Chapters 7 and 8.

Training gun or sheepdogs is a useful skill, which can be learnt by trial and error, by shadowing an experienced gun or sheepdog trainer, or by reading books on the subject. Often gun dog and sheepdog breeders train their own pups, with simple obedience training up to the age of about six months, then more task-specific training from six months upwards. A fully trained dog can then be sold on, and is quite valuable.

What training and experience are needed?
There is no single qualification that entitles you to act as a trainer, but there are numerous courses that are advertised, for example in *Dogs Today*. Unfortunately, there are no government

grants for funding this sort of training.

Experience of working with dogs is important to see how they behave normally, and to get used to handling them. It is useful to gain experience in boarding kennels or veterinary practices, either work shadowing or part-time employment. Joining a local training club is useful, preferably one with instructors certified by the British Institute of Professional Dog Trainers. The Kennel Club maintains a list of training clubs.

An alternative route to becoming a professional dog trainer is through charities and the Services' own training courses.

CASE STUDY

Graham Watkins, gundog trainer

Graham has been training gun dogs for 15 years. His academic qualifications include two A levels and five O levels, but rather than take specific courses in gundog training, his knowledge is derived from extensive experience working with dogs.

Graham starts work at 8 am. The first part of the morning is spent on kennel duties such as cleaning out and making sure a fresh supply of water is available. In the later part of the morning he gives private lessons to individuals, and then spends the afternoon training the residential dogs. At 5 pm the dogs are fed.

Graham also demonstrates gun dogs at major country events and shows. He finds it very rewarding to train the dog owners to become good handlers, but finds it demoralising trying to produce a good dog from poor starting material. His income is not high from the job, but he is happy with the working conditions and would choose the same career again.

CHARITY WORKER

There are many jobs, both paid and voluntary, caring for dogs within charities, such as the RSPCA and Guide Dogs for the Blind. These are discussed further in Chapter 8.

COMPETING WITH DOGS

Competition with dogs is usually a combination of breeding and training, which are both discussed elsewhere in this chapter. Three examples of competitions involving dogs are illustrated below.

What all three have in common is the lack of financial incentive to take up these sports – they might really be counted as hobbies rather than careers.

Sheepdog trials

Sheepdog trialling is familiar to many through the TV programme *One Man and his Dog*. The objective is to show the skill of a sheepdog by demonstrating its ability to round up a small number of sheep and manoeuvre them as directed by the shepherd. To succeed in this sport involves skill on the part of the dog and handler. The dog's skill comes partly from innate ability, and partly from intensive training by the handler.

Initially, the dog is given obedience training from the age of a few weeks. A dog that shows promise will begin specific training at between 6 and 12 months of age. The dog is taught to work with sheep, responding to commands from the shepherd in the form of whistles, hand signals and voice commands. The dog must be extremely obedient, obeying orders instantly, but must also have some degree of initiative to respond to the unexpected. It must have sufficient 'presence' to intimidate the sheep into doing what is required, but mustn't be aggressive or nervous. The skilled shepherd will spot these qualities in the youngster and nurture them.

Rewards for success are not high, but a well-trained sheepdog may sell for £1,500, and a champion triallist can be used as a breeding bitch or stud dog to obtain extra income.

Gun dog trials

Gun dog trialling has a lot in common with sheepdog trialling – rearing and training young dogs to compete in a specific sport. Again, specific training begins at 6–12 months of age, and again, the only real financial rewards are from selling trained gun dogs to field sports enthusiasts for approximately £1,500–£2,000 (compared to an untrained labrador of undistinguished pedigree selling for about £350), and from breeding trial champions.

Greyhound racing

Although not as large as the horse racing industry, there is a reasonable amount of money in greyhound racing by virtue of the betting associated with it. Profits from gambling usually go to the bookmakers rather than the racers and trainers unless they use their knowledge of the sport to place bets themselves, but there is a trickle-down effect so that prize money is higher than it would be without the betting industry.

Greyhounds are bred for speed and raised with this in mind. Their training is orientated towards physical fitness by means of diet and exercise, rather than obedience. There is a high wastage in the greyhound industry, for example those that aren't fast enough or become injured. Many are consequently humanely destroyed, although the RSPCA and greyhound rescue societies try to find homes for as many as they can, and there is a movement to try to breed from only the very best to lessen the production of substandard dogs who are of no use. Greyhounds do make remarkably good pets, despite often having had limited social experience, although they do have quirks. For example, some are scared of shiny floors, possibly because they never experience them until they have retired.

Financial rewards come from prize money, and from the use of dogs or bitches that have won races for breeding purposes. And to keep the breeders and racers going, there is always the dream of producing a dog like Miss Whirl, who held the National American Win Title in 1965 and became the first greyhound to earn more than $100,000.

BREEDING AND SHOWING DOGS AND CATS

Showing is another way of competing with animals, but the skill here lies in breeding examples that conform to breed standards set by the governing bodies such as the Kennel Club. All recognised dog and cat breeds have guidelines as to what is expected of a good specimen, such as size, colour, markings, build and shape of face. It should be noted that the guidelines are usually formulated for cosmetic reasons, and in the past, breeding for extreme features has been detrimental to breeds and to individual animals. One example is the bulldog, which has been bred with such a short nose that it has trouble breathing and cannot run far without getting out of breath.

Although breeding is involved in other types of competition than showing, it is vital to the showing process. Similarly, although it is possible to breed animals without ever showing, it is usually desirable to show good specimens, since prospective buyers like to know their animal is of good pedigree. Breeding and showing are thus dealt with together here.

The process starts with the selection of parents. The female (bitch for a dog, queen for a cat) is usually owned by the breeder. The male (stud) may or may not belong to the breeder, and more frequently belongs to someone else, since this allows a wider choice of genetic material. The bitch or queen is taken to the stud so mating takes place on the stud's territory. It is important that both parents are healthy and vaccinated to prevent the spread of disease.

The stud fee is usually payable to the owner if the female falls pregnant, and is an amount equivalent to the price of one puppy or kitten. Gestation lasts about nine weeks in dogs and cats. A large breeding establishment may try to have at least one animal pregnant all the time, to ensure a constant supply of puppies and kittens. There are legal guidelines as to how many litters a bitch may have, and to what age. A licence is required if two or more breeding bitches are kept. This is to prevent the abuse of the breeding animals by 'puppy farming', although the guidelines are loosely enforced and the practice continues.

Breeders' responsibilities

The pregnant animal needs special attention to diet, with increased feeding of high quality nutrients necessary in the latter stages of pregnancy. Birth should be closely supervised, even in the middle of the night, and problems may require veterinary attention. If the mother doesn't produce enough milk, the breeder may have to feed the young, which will initially be every two hours, even through the night!

It is the breeder's responsibility to worm the puppies or kittens. Vaccinations may be done by the breeder or by the new owners, depending on at what age they are sold. A good specimen may be retained by the breeder for further breeding or for showing.

Showing animals

An animal kept for showing may need basic obedience training, and must learn the elements of ringcraft. Shows exist for youngsters as well as for mature animals. In Crufts, the Kennel Club Show, categories are split by breed, by group (eg toy, utility, working) and an overall winner is designated. A prize at Crufts is well-respected, and allows a much higher price to be charged for the winner's offspring.

What qualifications or experience are needed?

No specific qualifications or training are required to breed and show, but advice from vets and breeders before starting is advisable, and reading around the subject and joining organisations such as the Kennel Club are also important. Breeders also need facilities in which to keep their animals, such as secure runs and heated kennels, together with essential equipment such as beds, first aid materials, artificial milk etc.

CASE STUDY

Vicki Clark, dog and cat breeder/shower

Vicki has been breeding dogs for 14 years and cats for six years, favouring oriental breed cats such as Siamese, and bearded collies. She has no qualifications specific to breeding or showing, but is a qualified veterinary nurse, and is head nurse at an Oxfordshire Veterinary Hospital.

The majority of her working time is spend on veterinary nursing, but she still has to spend time feeding, grooming her dogs and walking them at trotting speed to build up muscle. She regularly checks her animals' teeth, weight and muscle tone, and frequently baths the dogs.

The week before a show she bathes the dogs all over in shampoo to improve their coat texture and gives them a show groom (which takes approximately two hours). The night before the show she bathes the white parts in a whitening shampoo, and applies chalk if necessary. She carefully examines the cats, too, the night before they are shown, trimming their nails, checking their eyes, ears and teeth and giving them a bran bath.

Her most memorable experiences are from handling a home bred dog at Crufts, and winning an award with a home bred cat at the Supreme Show. She finds it very rewarding to breed healthy, good looking animals, and shows are a good chance to catch up with friends. However, the competitive nature of showing leads to jealousy from others, and she says that some would even go to the lengths of damaging other people's animals. That said, she would still choose the same career options again.

USEFUL ADDRESSES AND WEB SITES

British Dog Groomers Association, Bedford Business Centre, 170

Mile Road, Bedford MK42 9YZ. Tel: (01234) 273933.

British Greyhound Racing Board: www.thedogs.co.uk

British Institute of Professional Dog Trainers, Bowstone Gate, Nr Disley, Cheshire SK12 2AW.

Governing Council of Cat Fancy, 4–6 Penel Orlieu, Bridgwater, Somerset TA6 3PG.

The Kennel Club, 1–5 Clarges Street, Piccadilly, London W1Y 8AB.   www.the-kennel-club.org.uk   info@the-kennel-club.org.uk

National Association of Security Dog Users, Image House, Kingfield Road, Old Woking, Surrey GU22 9DZ. www.k9netuk.com

Petcare Trust, Bedford Business Centre, 170 Mile Road, Bedford MK42 9YZ. Tel: (01234) 273933. info@petcare.org.uk

FURTHER READING

Doglopedia, J. Evans and K. White (Henston).

Dogs Today (monthly periodical), Pankhurst Farm, Bagshot Road, West End, Nr Woking, Surrey GU24 9QR.

Grooming Dogs for Profit, C. Gold (Howell Book House).

The Reign of the Greyhound, C. Branigan (Howell Book House).

Running Your Own Boarding Kennels, Sheila Zabawa (Kogan Page).

Veterinary Notes for Dog Owners, T. and J. Turner (Stanley Paul).

6

Working in Agriculture

WHAT FARM WORK ENTAILS

Working on a farm often seems like a dream job to the city dweller: outdoor work; working with animals; low stress; no paperwork. But few make the transition from city to country, and few fully understand what a life in agriculture entails. There are several reasons people from towns don't move into farm work:

- Contrary to the general perception of farmers' incomes a decade ago, with good prices for produce swollen by subsidies, the general public realise the difficulties farmers now have to face, such as plummeting prices, loss of export markets and withdrawal of subsidies. Further, to set up in farming requires a considerable capital investment.

- Training and experience. Many believe that people are born to farming, rather than learning it. This is untrue. While being brought up on a farm undoubtedly has advantages, such as experience of animal husbandry and ease of employment (with family or other contacts), there are many courses teaching agricultural skills, and experience is easily gained by volunteering for farm work, especially at busy times of the year such as lambing or haymaking.

- Fear of the unknown. Farmers are often viewed as a race apart within the country, hostile towards the 'townie'. In general, farmers are irritated by those who express ill-informed views about the countryside, and those who damage their livelihood, such as people who trample crops or allow their dogs to worry sheep. But someone desiring to fit into the countryside and contribute to the rural way of life will usually find farmers neighbourly and welcoming.

● Working in agriculture is a broad topic, narrowed only slightly by limiting it to working with farm animals. However, all animal farming jobs have certain things in common. For example, they all involve a considerable amount of husbandry, ie day-to-day care, periodic health care and routine preventive medicine, planning and monitoring of breeding and birth, as well as less animal-orientated tasks such as Ministry of Agriculture paperwork, organising supplies of feed, tending fields, repairing farm buildings and machinery, and cleaning.

What training and experience are needed?

There are different routes into farming, from university degrees (see Appendix 1) to on-the-job training requiring no formal qualifications. No single route is necessarily superior to any other, and the choice depends upon the individual's ambitions. If one wants to take over the running of the family firm, then no specific qualifications are necessary, although college courses in agriculture and business management may be useful. If the aim is to run a farm or estate belonging to someone else, then qualifications such as an agriculture degree give a competitive edge. As with all animal jobs, experience counts. Farmers may take on casual labour or work experience students from the age of 16. The more experience the better. If you know the sort of job you are aiming for, for example in dairy farming, then target your experience towards this area. Experience in a pig unit will count for little if applying for a job milking cows. However, if you are unsure of your preferred field, then taking a variety of work experience placements can help you make up your mind.

Job prospects

The prospects for employment in agriculture currently aren't rosy. There are two reasons for this – the increased automation of farm tasks, and the decline in agriculture in the UK in general. However, there are some reasons for optimism. There are only so many tasks on a farm that can be entrusted to machines, and on a modern farm that limit is close to being reached. There will still be a considerable need for human input. Also, while farming is currently in its biggest slump for decades, it is likely that this will change in the medium term, with the BSE crisis all but resolved, and the government becoming more aware of the difficulties farmers face.

Farms usually specialise in a single species of animal, since this allows higher profitability by having increased expertise in rearing, and housing and pasture suited to this species. Some farms, though, have a mixed stock, the commonest being cattle and sheep. Farming of different species is described below.

CATTLE FARMING

Cattle farming can be broadly divided into two categories, dairy and beef. Dairy farming is mainly concerned with the production of milk, beef farming with the production of calves to be reared for meat. There is some overlap, however, with dairy cows being mated with beef bulls to ensure the supply of milk, while retaining some value in the calves, either if sold on or home-reared.

Dairy farms maintain a herd of cows for the production of milk. The aim is for them to produce one calf a year. Pregnancy is about nine months, milk is produced for about nine months after the calf is born. In the last three months of pregnancy the cow is 'dry' (ie not producing milk), while it puts its energy into growing the calf. A few days after birth the calf is removed from the mother and fed milk replacer, while the milk is taken from the cow two to three times daily for human consumption.

Various factors influence the profitability of a dairy farm. External factors include the price of milk (traditionally good, but lower since the ending of the monopoly of the Milk Marketing Board) and the price of calves, as well as fixed expenses such as rent and variable expenses such as food prices and vet bills. Internal profitability factors which can be influenced by the farmer include the cows' fertility (a complex parameter, affected by the cow's health, nutrition, genetics and milk production), output of milk and general health.

A typical day on a dairy farm involves an early start. Milking is usually done at 12-hour intervals, and can take a couple of hours to complete, so in order to finish afternoon milking by tea-time, the morning milking often starts at 4 am. The cows are brought into the milking parlour in rotation. Several are milked at once by automatic milking machines. The teats are cleaned, the milking machine is connected to the teats, and then removed when milking is complete. The cows are usually fed a concentrate ration while they are being milked. After milking, the teats are disinfected. Once all the cows have been milked the milking machine is disinfected, and the parlour cleaned out.

Other daily and periodic tasks, which are fitted in between milkings, include:

- maintenance of farm buildings

- ploughing, seeding and fertilising of fields

- harvesting of forage crops

- planning of fertility

- routine health tasks such as foot care, vaccinations and worming

- feeding of calves

- putting fresh litter down.

There are also occasions when the farmer has to drop everything, for example to attend a sick animal, or help a cow with a difficult calving. Cows have the nasty habit of calving in the middle of the night, which can make cattle farming a 24-hour job. If the farmer intends to be away from the farm for a significant period, he or she will need to employ someone to keep an eye on the animals.

Beef farming is essentially similar to dairy farming, but the milk from the cows is used to rear calves. The only source of income on the beef farm is from the sale of cattle, usually shortly before they reach the age of 30 months (currently in the UK, cattle over the age of 30 months cannot be sold for human consumption). Although the income from beef farming is consequently lower than on a dairy farm, the outgoings are a lot lower. The amount of labour required is lower because there is no need for the time-consuming milking. There is also no need to buy and maintain the expensive milking machine. Furthermore, beef cattle tend to be slightly healthier than dairy cattle due to the lower demands placed on their body systems, so vet bills are often lower.

For the above reasons, many farmers abandoned dairy farming in recent years in favour of beef farming. At the height of the BSE crisis in the mid to late 1990s beef prices fell considerably, but are showing some signs of recovery, and 'finished' beef (ie ready to go to market) sells reasonably well.

Because of the low labour requirements of beef farming, jobs are few and far between, and most beef farms are run by their owners.

SHEEP FARMING

There are two main sources of income for sheep farmers, meat and wool. The sale of fleeces after shearing used to contribute substantially to the sheep farmer's finances. However, modern fabrics have led to a decrease in demand for wool, so most sheep farmers concentrate on breeds that produce good quality meat. A few farmers sell sheep milk for human consumption, but the market for this is low.

Sheep farming is usually divided into hill farming and lowland farming. Lowland farming utilises good quality land, often improved by drainage and fertilising to allow a relatively large number of sheep to be kept in a relatively small area. Hill farming involves little or no pasture care, and the sheep are allowed to roam extensively, finding grazing where they can.

Lowland farming has several advantages over hill farming. By keeping the sheep in a smaller area, they can be more closely supervised, allowing routine healthcare and administrative tasks to be performed more easily. Extra feed is easily supplied to pregnant and lactating ewes and the better health and nutrition allows the farmer to achieve a higher 'lambing percentage' (the number of live lambs produced per ewe) and better growth rates of the young lambs. However, there are some advantages to hill farming. Since for the most part the sheep are left to their own devices, the labour input is lower. The land is usually remote and of little value for anything else, agricultural or otherwise, and so is cheap to rent or buy. Furthermore, there are subsidies available for keeping sheep in certain areas, since they contribute to conservation by their grazing. Many subsidies are being phased out, however, so this cannot be relied upon in the long term.

The tasks a sheep farmer has to carry out vary with the season.

The rams are put in with the ewes in summer or autumn, depending on when lambing is planned. They must be in good health before this (feet trimmed, good body condition, etc), since they will have to work hard! The farmer ensures that all the ewes are mated, and may bring in an ultrasound scanner to check the ewes are pregnant, and how many lambs they are carrying, so feeding levels can be adjusted accordingly.

Lambing takes place in winter or spring and may be synchronised into one or two tight batches, or spread out. There is usually a month in which extremely close supervision of the lambing ewes is required. There is a saying that sheep are born with a will to die, and will try many ingenious methods of 'suicide', from being suffocated by their own birth membranes, to drowning themselves in water troughs, being caught by foxes, developing diseases such as 'watery mouth', or dropping dead for no apparent reason. The diligence and skill of the farmer and his or her employees greatly influence the size of the lamb crop that will be obtained.

There is therefore a month of sleepless nights, assisting with difficult lambings and treating sick lambs and ewes. Other tasks at lambing time include:

- feeding ewes

- cleaning out to maintain good hygiene

- applying rubber rings to the lambs for castration and tail docking

- numbering lambs for identification

- feeding orphan or rejected lambs

- turning out lambs when they are old enough

- vaccinating against pasteurella and clostridial diseases

- foot trimming of ewes.

As spring gives way to summer, the number of sheep left to lamb drops off dramatically, and it is possible to catch up on lost sleep. The workload is a lot less in the summer than spring, but there are still many tasks to be performed, including keeping fencing secure (sheep are great escapologists), sorting out ewes who will not be bred from in the following year and taking them to market, along with the spring's crop of lambs when they have reached the correct age and weight. In late summer or autumn the process starts again.

Sheep farming can be rewarding, and also depressing, for example if disease takes a larger number of lambs than expected, or if the ewes produce many single lambs and few twins. Sheep prices are currently very low, and sadly many sheep farmers are going out of business, but hopefully the situation will improve in the future.

CASE STUDY

Caroline Morris, general farm worker

Caroline helped on her father's farm from a young age, gaining knowledge and experience from her father and uncle. She went to university and graduated with a BSc (Hons) in health science. For the last three years she has been working on the family farm, a mixed dairy and sheep farm. Caroline works with both species, but is particularly responsible for the sheep.

From February to March Caroline helps with lambing on a neighbour's farm, but from March she is needed back at home, with their own sheep due to lamb. In March and April she checks the sheep in the field daily, using her quad bike to take feed out to them. At the beginning of March, all the sheep are vaccinated. One or two groups are injected per day over a five-day period. At the end of March the sheds are prepared for lambing. This involves erecting pens for the ewes with newly born lambs, and positioning of feeders.

Come April and May it is non-stop lambing from dawn to dusk and beyond. Caroline stays in the lambing shed all day, while someone else checks the lambs and sheep that are out in the fields. She moves sheep that have lambed into individual pens and feeds and waters them. Sheep that lamb outside are brought in by the quad bike and penned. After 24-hours she marks them for identification and releases them, either outside if the weather is good enough, or into bigger pens with several sheep in if the weather is poor. Hay and water is provided for all sheep and she also feeds concentrate pellets.

In May and June Caroline is still lambing, but things are slackening off now. She still goes round the fields daily to check lambs and ewes are well. In the middle of May all the sheep are shorn by contractors, which usually takes a week. In mid-June the lambs are weaned.

All the lambs and sheep that are to be sold go to a local sheep fair, which is held on the first Friday and Saturday of August, so towards the end of July the sheep are sorted into matching groups of about 25–30 and marked so they are ready for the market. This takes roughly a week. The ewes are dipped for sheep scab before they are sold.

If all the sheep are sold at market, Caroline enjoys some time of relative peace and quiet, with just the cattle to worry about. It doesn't last long though. In the second or third week of August they start buying in ewe lambs. More are purchased in October. In September all the new acquisitions are shorn by a contractor, weather permitting. In November the sheep are placed on other farms for winter grazing. Before this can be done Caroline and others have to put up electric fencing. The rams are then put in, and the owner of the farm the sheep are on keeps an eye on them. Caroline goes out every one or two weeks to check everything is well.

In January to February the sheep come home, and the electric wire has to be rolled up. The sheep are all scanned for pregnancy by ultrasound, and then sorted into different lambing stages. Caroline then braces herself for lambing to start anew.

One of Caroline's most memorable experiences is developing a severe allergy to rubber lamb castration rings which caused her hands, arms and face to become red, swollen and painful. It took doctors four weeks to discover the problem! She finds it rewarding, however, treating sick sheep and lambs and seeing them back in the field when they are better. It is also satisfying when the sheep and lambs sell well at market. Market prices have been low this last year though, so recently that hasn't been the case.

More disheartening aspects of the job include going out into a field and finding something dead for no apparent reason. She also finds it sad to work hard to manage a large flock well, only to find there isn't a big enough market. It is hard, she says, to still have the enthusiasm for looking after sheep properly when it seems she is producing something no one wants. She would still choose the same job again, and finds the working conditions, career prospects and status in the public eye satisfactory. However, her earnings are quite low.

PIG FARMING

Pigs are bred almost solely for meat, in the form for example of gammon, bacon or pork. There are no subsidies in the pig farming industry, so each farmer stands or falls depending on his business acumen, farming skills and other factors such as market prices. The pig business went through a good period in the 1980s with reasonably high prices for bacon. However, it is currently struggling. One of the reasons for this is the tightening by the UK government of welfare regulatons. Sows used to be kept tethered or confined in stalls without enough room to turn around. In a post-war Britain hungry for food, the reasoning was sound. By preventing the pigs from exercising, less energy was wasted and more of the food turned directly into meat, or milk for the piglets. Furthermore, it prevented the sow from damaging the piglets by lying on them or even attacking them. However, this was shown by scientific study to cause the pigs distress and psychological problems, and so stalls and tethers were banned in the UK in 1998, forcing farmers to spend money on new housing systems (for which no government grants were available). Unfortunately, such guidelines are not in force in other countries, even within the EU, allowing them to produce bacon more cheaply and undercut the British prices.

Pigs may be kept indoors or outdoors. Most indoor sows are now loose-housed in straw-bedded barns. Sophisticated feeding methods exist, including electronic collars, which dispense measured amounts of food from an automatic feeder to individual sows. The sows are taken to the boar's pen when they are on heat. The boars are housed individually, since they are aggressive and dangerous, both to humans and other pigs.

The sow is often scanned by ultrasound to check if she is pregnant. When she is due to farrow, she is moved to an individual pen. Sows produce lots of small piglets and hence tend to give birth more easily than cows and sheep, which produce small numbers of large young. Hence farrowing doesn't require as close supervision as lambing or calving. Measures need to be taken, however, to prevent the sow savaging or lying on the piglets. A separate area with a heat lamp is usually provided, which only the piglets can get into. Soon after birth the piglets have their teeth clipped to prevent damage to the sow's teats. Preventative medications may be given.

Once they are weaned, the piglets are moved into other pens. Mixing of different litters needs to be supervised, since fights frequently break out to determine the pecking order. The piglets are put into groups of roughly equal weight, so feeding is easier, and the situation of runts being prevented from reaching the food is avoided. As they become older they are called 'weaners,' 'growers' and finally 'finishers' before going to market.

Part of the pig farmer's duties involves removing the copious amounts of manure that the pigs produce. There are also feeding and administrative tasks such as tagging or tattooing, planning of breeding and taking pigs to market. High standards of hygiene are usually maintained to prevent the spread of diseases from other pigs into the herd.

There is a growing trend to keep pigs out of doors. This is perceived as being more welfare-friendly, although plenty of shelter must be provided, since the hairless pigs sunburn in the summer and chill in the winter. It is more difficult to catch and handle the pigs outside, so this is done less often. There is also less manure-shovelling! However, production is usually less efficient, so although money is saved on housing and heating, less income is generated since fewer pigs survive to finishing, and they are usually of a lower weight.

RARE BREEDS AND OPEN FARMS

There is another method of farming which increases income, and that is to open the farm to paying members of the public in a similar manner to running a zoo. The difference between an open farm and a zoo, however, is that the open farm is usually a working proposition, and animals are still sent to market. The extra income gained from admission fees helps to maintain the viability of the business, and allows the farm to diversify in ways that otherwise wouldn't be possible. One example of this is to keep rare breeds of farm animals. Rare breeds are traditional breeds that were once commonplace in the British countryside. However, they have been superseded by breeds, often imported from

Europe, that have better production values such as fertility, food conversion ratios and milk yield. It is important not to allow these rare breeds to die out, since they carry genetic material that may be of great use in the future. When they are gone, they are gone forever. Fortunately, many rare breeds such as the Gloucester Old Spot pig, the Soay sheep and the British White cow make attractive show pieces and so are ideal for the open farm.

Duties on an open farm are essentially the same as on an ordinary farm, but the farm workers must remember that everything they do is subject to scrutiny from the public. Thus they must be friendly and happy to talk to people. They must also treat the animals with extreme consideration – handling and husbandry practices must be beyond reproach.

There are rewarding aspects to working on an open farm, and seeing the faces of children when a new lamb is born reminds the most cynical what a miracle it is!

AM I SUITED TO A CAREER IN AGRICULTURE?

If you are considering this career, you should ask yourself the following questions:

- Am I prepared to get my hands dirty? Farming animals requires a large amount of hands-on work, often in mud or worse. After a period of time dirt often becomes ingrained under the nails and in the fingers and won't come out even with a long soak in the bath.

- Am I physically fit? Much farm work requires physical effort, such as walking, mucking out and animal handling. Any health problems or disabilities that impair your ability to perform manual labour may be a serious disadvantage.

- Am I prepared to work outdoors in all weathers? Farmers have to work outside most of the time, whether it be harvesting on a sweltering summer's day, or feeding sheep in the middle of a snowy January.

- Am I sentimental towards animals in my care? Most animals on farms are kept purely for their usefulness and profitability.

Many are raised to produce meat, but even those that are kept for their produce, such as milking cows, are rarely retained after they can no longer perform the function they were kept for. If you get over-attached to animals, farming may not be the job for you.

USEFUL ADDRESSES AND WEB SITES

Berkshire College of Agriculture (see Chapter 2).
Ministry of Agriculture, Fisheries and Food (see Chapter 2).
National Farmer's Union, 164 Shaftesbury Avenue, London WC2H 8HL. www.nfu.org.uk
Somerset Cattle Breeding Centre, Horlicks Farms and Dairies, Hort Bridge, Ilminster, Somerset TA19 9PR.
University of Reading, Whiteknights, PO Box 217, Reading RG6 6AH. schools.liaison@rdg.ac.uk (offers agriculture related degrees).
Young Farmers' Club, National Agricultural Centre, Stoneleigh Park, Kenilworth, Warwickshire CV8 2LG. www.nfyfc.org.uk

FURTHER READING

The Principles of Dairy Farming, K. Slater (Farming Press).
Farmers Weekly, Reed Business Publishing, Quadrant House, The Quadrant, Sutton, Surrey SM2 5AS.

7

Working in the Services

The police, Her Majesty's Customs and Excise and the Armed Forces all make use of animals to aid in their duties. The main species used is the dog which, with its adaptability, trainability and keen senses, can be used for a variety of roles. These include:

- patrol/guard duties

- sniffer dogs to search for guns, explosives and drugs

- search and rescue duties

- apprehension of criminals.

Horses are mainly used for crowd control and ceremonial duties.

WORKING WITH CUSTOMS AND EXCISE

Job description

HM Customs and Excise employs 23,000 people around the UK and is concerned with collection of VAT and business duties, as well as working to prevent drug smuggling and trade in other illegal goods. The Customs Detector Dog Service is the branch of the department involved with the use of dogs to detect and prevent drug smuggling.

The dogs are used to pinpoint the location of drugs, either carried about the smuggler's person, in baggage or in freight. All the dogs are trained (at the Defence Animal Centre in Melton Mowbray) to detect heroin, cocaine, amphetamines and cannabis. There are roughly 90 dogs working at various ports and airports in the UK, and in 1997–98 they were associated with the seizing of £78 million worth of drugs.

The breeds used are usually gun dogs such as labradors and English springer spaniels. To train a sniffer dog takes six months. The standards are high, and many do not make the grade. The dogs do not consume the drugs, but are trained by receiving a reward when they scent a narcotic. Passive response dogs are trained to sit in the presence of drugs, while pro-active dogs find and retrieve drugs.

The dog handler is responsible for the day-to-day care of the sniffer dog, such as feeding, cleaning and exercising. At least two hours per day are spent on these tasks. The dogs are kept in department kennels and do not live at home with their handlers. However, when they retire their handlers often adopt them. If this is not possible, there is a list of people interested in adopting retired sniffer dogs.

What qualifications and experience are needed?
Sniffer dog handlers are only recruited from within the department's own ranks. The minimum entry requirements are five grade Cs at GCSE, one of which must be English language, and the age range for recruitment is 16 to 59. It would be sensible if you intend to enter Customs and Excise in order to become a dog handler to gain some experience working with dogs, such as in a boarding kennel. A handler should be flexible, a good team worker and a good communicator. It is also necessary to be fairly agile, since it is sometimes necessary to work in cramped conditions.

WORKING FOR THE POLICE

Job description
The police use dogs in various capacities for various tasks. These include:

- search and rescue

- searching for explosives and drugs

- crowd control

- apprehension of criminals

- tracking.

The majority of police dogs are German shepherds, obtained either by donation from the public or direct from breeders. The dogs are trained in standard obedience techniques, and then spend 13 weeks at a regional training centre learning the specific skills necessary for police work. At various points in the dog's life, he or she will have further training to reinforce and improve those skills.

The dogs are then assigned to handlers. The handler will have one dog, which he or she will keep at home and take into work every day. A close attachment usually forms between handler and dog, and when it is time for the dog to retire, the handler usually adopts the dog into their own home. It must be remembered, though, that the dogs are often required to go into dangerous situations, for example to tackle a criminal with a knife, and they can get injured or even killed.

It is general policy for an officer to serve with only one dog for its working life (about 6 years), before moving on to other duties within the force, although skilled handlers may apply to work with a second dog when the first retires.

What training and experience are needed?

Police dog handlers are chosen from within the ranks of existing police officers, on application from the individual. To join the police force an applicant must be aged between 18 years 3 months and 55 years, physically fit and competent with the English language. It is also necessary to pass an entrance test.

It is usual to complete approximately six years' service before applying to become a police dog handler. The applicant's work record to date is taken into consideration, as well as the suitability of his or her home environment to accommodate a police dog, such as possessing a large enough garden.

WORKING IN THE ARMY

The best chance of working with animals in the army is serving with the Royal Army Veterinary Corps (RAVC). The RAVC is the body responsible for the provision and care of the army's animals which mainly consist of dogs (for patrol, search and guard duties) and horses (largely ceremonial nowadays). The training of dogs is mainly handled by the Defence Animal Centre in Melton Mowbray.

There are various jobs within the RAVC, and they may hold a commissioned or a non-commissioned rank.

Veterinary surgeon

To join the RAVC as a veterinary surgeon, it is necessary to be licensed to practise as a veterinary surgeon in the UK, ie to be a Member of the Royal College of Veterinary Surgeons (MRCVS). Entry to the RCVS is by possession of a qualifying veterinary degree (see Chapter 2 for details). Experience of general practice after qualification and before joining the RAVC is beneficial. It is useful to have had a job dealing with both dogs and horses.

A qualified veterinary surgeon enters the RAVC as a commissioned officer, either a lieutenant or captain, depending on previous experience. Pay is commensurate with experience. In April 1999 the pay range was £20,068 to £22,170 per annum for a lieutenant, and £25,583 to £28,744 as a captain.

As an officer of the British Army, the veterinary surgeon in the RAVC needs certain skills and abilities above and beyond those required for his or her veterinary role. Officers should possess:

● leadership qualities

● teamwork abilities

● the ability to earn respect

● physical fitness

● the ability to think and react quickly.

Non-commissioned jobs

Applicants to the RAVC start with an interview at a regional Army Careers Information Office. There is then a medical examination, an entrance exam and a period of assessment at the Defence Animal Centre. Successful applicants are enlisted into the RAVC, and go on for basic training lasting 14 weeks. Further training for all recruits consists of three two-week courses on patrol dog handling, stable management and veterinary first aid. Following this, successful recruits are divided up for training specific to the trade they will follow with the RAVC. These are described below.

Veterinary technician

The veterinary technician plays a similar role in the RAVC to the veterinary nurse in private practice. Tasks performed include:

- monitoring anaesthetics

- assisting in surgery

- taking and developing x-rays

- performing laboratory procedures such as blood tests

- first aid for injured/sick animals

- general nursing and supportive tasks

- teaching other RAVC personnel.

Training takes 13 weeks, and is based at the Services Veterinary Hospital. Once this is complete the rank of lance-corporal is usually awarded. Further promotion is possible up to the rank of sergeant, and it is even possible to get a commission as an officer.

The RAVC qualification as veterinary technician is not officially recognised outside the RAVC, but on leaving the army there is a chance for employment in a veterinary practice as a non-qualified veterinary nurse (although certain restrictions apply as to which tasks may be carried out). It is also possible to work in practice management or as a sales rep for a drug company.

Dog trainer

Army dog trainers train service dogs for various tasks, but predominantly for guard duties and search/detection role, such as sniffing out explosives and drugs. One trainer may train up to six dogs at a time, and during that time the trainer will be responsible for the dogs' general care, husbandry and welfare. The recruit progresses through three classes, from Class 3 to Class 1. The courses cover animal husbandry, kennel management and dog training. On completion of the specialist training, the rank of lance corporal is usually awarded. Over time it is possible to rise through the ranks, and even get a commission and become an officer.

Upon leaving the army, there are many opportunities to continue working with dogs, for example for private security firms, the police and the prison service. Although the RAVC qualification is not formally recognised in civilian life, ex-RAVC trainers are acknowledged to be of high calibre and are consequently sought after.

Farrier

Farriers are required to attend to the feet of the army's horses. Although the modern army horses fulfil largely ceremonial roles, they need to be sound to perform their duties and the farrier, in conjunction with the veterinary officer, helps ensure this by appropriate shoeing and shaping of the foot. More details of the job of farriery can be found in Chapter 4, and your local Army Recruitment Office can also provide information.

PRISON DOG HANDLER

Job description

Dogs have been used in prisons since 1967 to assist prison wardens. They have various roles, including patrolling, searching, interception and deterrence. Specialised dogs are also used to search for drugs, explosives and firearms. Most patrol dogs are German shepherds, while the 'sniffer' dogs are mainly labradors and springer spaniels. The dogs are donated by members of the public or bought from breeders. The prison dog handler keeps the dog in his own home when it is off duty, and will often adopt it when it retires.

What qualities and experience are needed?

New prison dog handlers are drawn from the ranks of existing prison officers. To become a prison officer it is necessary to be at least 20 years old, and to possess five GCSEs at Grade C or above, including Maths and English language.

After serving a one-year probationary period, it is possible for a prison officer to apply to become a prison dog handler. Selection is by interview, with consideration for past record, ability to look after a dog at home, reliability and stability. A successful candidate undergoes an eight-week training course.

Job prospects

A patrol dog handler usually earns a salary in the region of £16,000 to £21,000. Disciplined drug dog handlers may earn more. Promotion is possible from Officer Dog Handler to Dog Section Manager, to Principal Officer, but the job becomes more administrative as higher ranks are reached.

USEFUL ADDRESSES AND WEBSITES

Armed Forces Career Offices: www.army.mod.uk (Consult *Yellow Pages* for your local branch).

British Police and Services Canine Association, PO Box 2078, Edgbaston, Birmingham B16 8QZ.

Her Majesty's Customs and Excise: www.hmce.gov.uk

8

Working for Charities

There are a large number of animal-orientated charities based in the UK. These can be broadly categorised into those whose aim is to help animals – the welfare charities, and those that use animals to help humans – the assistance charities.

Charities are funded by donations from members of the public, together with the income from investments they have, and occasionally from National Lottery grants. Donations come in the form of subscriptions from members, bequests in wills, collections on streets and in shops, and fund-raising activities of supports such as sponsored events. Often finances are stretched, with constant demands on budget from worthy causes. In order to ensure that limited resources are applied where they are needed, charities use a large number of voluntary workers and if earning a salary is not important to you, for example if your spouse is already earning a good wage, then there are plenty of opportunities in this field.

However, charities do employ salaried staff for various tasks, and though the wages are unlikely to be high, again due to limited resources, they usually provide a liveable income.

A range of charities is listed below and described, together with job opportunities.

WORKING FOR WELFARE CHARITIES

RSPCA

The RSPCA is one of the largest charities in the UK, with 207 branches in England and Wales. The SSPCA is the Scottish equivalent. The aim of the RSPCA is to prevent cruelty to animals, but this can be expressed in a variety of ways, from bringing prosecutions against those believed to be directly cruel or negligent to their own or other people's animals, to political campaigning, for example to ban fox hunting. The RSPCA also has veterinary hospitals for treatment of animals whose owners cannot afford to pay veterinary fees, wildlife centres for sick or injured animals and birds, and welfare centres for strays and animals that have been taken from their owners for cruelty, or given into the RSPCA's care due to the owners' inability or unwillingness to look after them.

There are various jobs within the RSPCA that involve hands-on work with animals.

RSPCA Inspector: job description

The RSPCA Inspectors probably have the most high-profile jobs in the RSPCA. They are responsible for a variety of tasks and duties, orientated towards helping animals in need and preventing cruelty or suffering to animals. Specific duties include:

- rescuing trapped or stuck animals

- investigating complaints of cruelty notified by members of the public, vets or police

- prosecuting those believed guilty of cruelty to animals

- inspecting premises that house animals

- administering first aid to sick or injured animals

- advising owners of animals.

Sometimes it is necessary to work unsociable hours, since the RSPCA provide a 24-hour emergency service. The work can be demanding, and may be depressing and rewarding in equal measures. For example, it can be distressing to find a litter of abandoned pups, malnourished and flea-ridden, but very satisfying to see them nursed back to health.

There is a lot of outdoor work involved, such as rounding up strays or rescue work, and some rescues may involve personal risk, either from the animal or the location, such as a cliff. A lot of time is spent working with people, including pet owners and members of the public, as well as other professionals with whom it may be necessary to liaise, such as vets, police and the Fire Brigade.

What qualifications and experience are needed?

Inspectors need to have a genuine interest and concern for animal welfare. They need to be prepared to work hard and for long hours, and must not be squeamish. Good communication skills are important. To enter the RSPCA you need to be aged 22–40, and possess GCSEs or O levels in English language and a science subject. You should be physically fit, and need to be capable of swimming for 50 metres fully clothed. You will also need a full driving licence.

Previous experience working with animals is useful, and since it is possible to be posted anywhere in England or Wales (or Scotland if joining the SSPCA), experience with a range of species, large and small, is preferable.

Successful applicants undergo a six-month training course at RSPCA HQ in Horsham, West Sussex. Subjects covered include:

- animal welfare legislation

- basic veterinary skills

- animal handling

- rescue techniques

- public speaking.

The course is followed by a written examination, then a 12-month probationary period, before full Inspector status is awarded.

Job prospects

The RSPCA employs about 300 Inspectors, but have only about 25 vacancies a year, for which there are hundreds of applicants. Salaries start from £10,380, with an experienced Inspector earning approximately £15,000 to £18,000 plus overtime. Promotion to higher grades or specialist positions is possible.

Other jobs at the RSPCA

Other positions working with animals at the RSPCA include:

- veterinary surgeon (see Chapter 2)

- veterinary nurse (see Chapter 2)

- kennel assistant

- hospital/clinic assistant.

There are also various non animal-orientated posts such as press officers, secretaries and administrators.

PDSA

The People's Dispensary for Sick Animals has clinics and hospitals throughout the country. Their aim is to provide veterinary care for animals whose owners cannot affort to pay for treatment. Criteria for providing care are strict, and usually evidence is required that the owner is in receipt of state benefits. Once accepted however, virtually all treatment is free, although the PDSA will not provide preventative treatment such as vaccinations and flea control products.

Job opportunities are mainly for veterinary surgeons and veterinary nurses, and although the PDSA is a charity supported entirely by public donation, the rates of pay are reasonable, and the clinics are often well-equipped. For more information about careers as a veterinary surgeon or veterinary nurse, see Chapter 2.

Cats' Protection League

Established in 1927, the Cats' Protection League is the UK's oldest cat welfare charity. Their main concern is rescue of abandoned and stray cats and cats whose owners can no longer look after them for reasons such as divorce, redundancy or disability. The CPL has 14 purpose-built shelters and over 240 branches throughout the UK, and together they are responsible for rescuing 75,000 cats per year. Despite this, resources are still stretched, and to have a cat waiting for a position for every two cats in care is not an uncommon situation.

Each of the 14 shelters employs a small number of paid staff, but the vast majority of those working for CPL are unpaid volunteers. Volunteers perform a range of tasks such as:

- fund-raising

- home visits

- fostering cats in specially built garden pens

- transporting cats, eg to new homes or to the vet.

Donkey Sanctuary
The Donkey Sanctuary became a registered charity in 1973, and aims to provide a home for donkeys which have been neglected or can no longer be looked after by the owners. Most of these are cared for at the Sanctuary's main premises near Sidmouth in Devon. There are also many donkeys fostered out to people throughout the country who have the time and space to care for them properly.

The Donkey Sanctuary employs staff to care for the donkeys, nurse sick animals under veterinary supervision and perform general husbandry duties, as well as transport donkeys that need rescuing from around the country to the Donkey Sanctuary.

International League for Protection of Horses
The ILPH was founded in 1927, with the objective of safeguarding the welfare of the horses being exported from the UK to Europe for slaughter. It has grown into the world's top equine welfare charity.

The ILPH has five recovery and rehabilitation centres in the UK, including Hill Farm in Snetterton, Norfolk, and Cherry Tree Farm in Lingfield, Surrey. At any one time the ILPH is caring for roughly 300 horses. The charity also employs 15 full-time field officers, mainly former police officers. Their duties include:

- investigation of reports of cruelty or neglect

- inspection of markets and ports

- monitoring horses loaned to fosterers.

The ILPH aims to rehabilitate every horse coming into its care, provided prolonging life does not cause further suffering. If a horse is capable of an active life, the charity tries to place it with a suitable owner, although the ILPH retains responsibility for these horses.

National Canine Defence League
The NCDL is the UK's largest dog welfare charity. Its aims are to prevent cruelty, abandonment and neglect to all dogs, at home and abroad. The charity goes about this by education and welfare campaigns, coupled with Rehoming Centres throughout the country. The NCDL believes that no healthy dog should be destroyed.

Blue Cross
The Blue Cross aims to help animals whose owners cannot afford veterinary treatment, promote animal welfare by education and find homes for unwanted animals. It does this through its three veterinary hospitals, one veterinary clinic, 11 adoption centres and two equine centres.

CASE STUDY

Monica Hornsey, Thames Valley Animal Welfare Co-ordinator, Treasurer, fosterer, editor of newsletter, etc. . .
Monica has been in her current, multi-faceted job, working for the animal rescue charity Thames Valley Animal Welfare, for seven years. She possesses a BA (Hons), but has found her knowledge and skills acquired whilst working more helpful, especially when dealing with people. She also has some knowledge of law and accounting which has come in handy.

Her daily routine starts with feeding the cats in her care, cleaning out their litter trays, and giving medication to those that require it. Then she has to turn her attention to administrative tasks. These include answering the phone, dealing with correspondence, placing adverts, accounting and liaising with the charity's 20 foster homes. She also keeps a close eye on the waiting list so she can take in the most desperate cats and kittens as soon as space becomes available.

In the evening Monica again feeds the cats and cleans out the litter trays, and every week she cleans and disinfects the cat houses and runs. She also regularly writes the newsletter for the Friends of TVAW, and attends fund-raising events. It is also important for her to liaise with vets – the charity has accounts with 11 practices used by their fosterers regularly, plus contact with 20 others in the area. She also produces publicity material, and reports to the Charities Commission.

Monica finds it very rewarding that they find homes for up to

400 cats and kittens every year, and it is even more rewarding if the rehomed cat had been sick or in their care for a long time. Their record so far is rehoming a cat after it had spent 18 months with them.

However, certain members of the public can make her work difficult, and it is also difficult being under constant pressure to find homes for cats, even having to turn some away, not knowing what will happen to them. The cats she sees each year, albeit small in number, that have suffered cruelty or neglect are also distressing.

Monica gains no income from her job. In fact, she comments, it seems to work the other way round! The public react to her in various ways, but most, she believes, view her as a saint or a fool! But in general she finds the job very satisfying.

WORKING FOR ASSISTANCE CHARITIES

Guide Dogs for the Blind Association
The first guide dogs in the UK were trained in 1931, and since then they have become a familiar sight on Britain's streets. The GDBA is primarily concerned with the provision, training and support of guide dogs for the visually impaired. However, it also provides other services for the blind and partially sighted, such as training them to get about with a long cane instead of a guide dog and learning to use such aids as Braille books and special magnifiers.

The GDBA has seven training centres throughout the country, employing a variety of staff.

Guide Dog Trainers and Guide Dog Mobility Instructors: Job description
Guide Dog Trainers start working with trainee guide dogs after the young dogs have spent about a year with volunteer puppy walkers (see below).

The trainers spend the first few weeks settling the dogs in at the training centre and assessing their suitability. They are then taught basic commands such as left, right, forwards and back. Further training teaches them to sit at roadsides and not cross when traffic is approaching, and teaches working in a harness.

In the last few months of training the dog is taken over by the Guide Dog Mobility Instructor, who teaches more advanced skills. These include such tasks as guiding through a crowd without bumping into anyone. The mobility instructor then pairs a visu-ally-impaired person with an appropriate dog. The instructor also teaches new owners how to work with their new animal, and helps them to gain confidence in handling the dog and coping in diffi-cult situations.

After the dog has been homed with a new owner, the instruc-tor makes periodic visits to ensure no problems have arisen, and to give help and support if needed.

What qualifications and experience are needed?

The minimum entry requirement to work as a Guide Dog Instructor is three GCSEs grade A–C, of which one must be English language. For a Guide Dog Mobility Instructor, five GCSEs grade A–C are required, which must include English, maths, a science and preferably a social science subject.

Both positions require excellent physical health and fitness and a clean driving licence. The minimum age for entry is 18 years. Experience working with people as well as with animals is useful, and strong interpersonal skills are important.

Guide dog trainers spend two months learning basic dog care and husbandry, then 11 months working for the City and Guilds qualification of Guide Dog Trainer. Guide Dog Mobility Instructors serve a three-year modular apprenticeship which leads to the GDBA Guide Dog Mobility qualification.

Prospects and pay

Competition is high for places – the Association receives approx-imately 100 queries per week, but only takes on 16–20 apprentices per year. Guide Dog Trainers' salaries start from about £9,000, ris-ing to £12,000 on qualifying, with a ceiling of about £14,000. Guide Dog Mobility Instructors begin on about £13,500 as an apprentice, rising to £19,500 after qualifying. Working hours are largely socia-ble, although there is some evening and weekend work. There is also an initial six-month live-in period for new Trainers and Instructors, during which accommodation and food are provided.

Guide Dog Trainers may be promoted to Senior Guide Dog Trainers or Puppy Walking Supervisors, and Mobility Instructors can be promoted to managerial posts, although this may involve less contact with the dogs.

Kennel staff

The GDBA employs staff responsible for the general care and husbandry of the dogs in its training centres. See Chapter 5 for further details on kennel worker duties.

Puppy socialiser/puppy walker

The GDBA enlists the help of volunteer puppy walkers to care for potential guide dogs through the important ages of six weeks to one year. During this period the pups are too immature to undergo formal training. However, they need to gain confidence and experience with the world at large, and their experiences in the first few months greatly affect their confidence and abilities later in life.

For this reason, the GDBA places puppies with volunteers to accustom them to a wide range of situations, such as crowds, traffic, children and other animals. Time is also spent with the puppies teaching basic obedience, exercising and playing.

At about one year of age the puppy is returned to the Guide Dog Centre for formal training. It can be difficult for the puppy walker to part with the puppy, but it is with the knowledge that if it passes its training, it will provide a lifetime of invaluable service to a blind person.

There is no financial reward for puppy walking, but the GDBA covers feeding expenses and vet bills as well as supplying basic equipment and giving advice when needed. The main requirements for puppy walking are:

● access to a car

● a secure, fenced garden

● not being away from home for more than three hours a day

● ideally having children of school age in the family.

Hearing Dogs for the Deaf

The Hearing Dog Scheme was launched in 1982 and the first training centre was set up in Chinnor in Oxfordshire. In Britain, 200 people in 1,000 suffer from a significant hearing loss. Of these, about 85 are potential Hearing Dog recipients. The dogs are trained to be the ears for the deaf person, hearing everyday sounds, then communicating by touch to guide the person to the source of the sound. The sound may be a door bell or phone, an alarm clock, a smoke alarm or a cooker timer. Suitable recipients have a severe hearing loss, are physically and financially able to care for a dog and can demonstrate a genuine need for a dog, such as living alone.

The Hearing Dog Scheme currently has two training centres, one in Lewknor in Oxfordshire, one in Cliffe, North Yorkshire. Further expansion is planned. Hearing Dogs for Deaf People employ staff in a number of roles.

Hearing Dog Trainer

Hearing Dog Trainers train up to five dogs at once. They take responsibility for them when they start at the centre after being looked after by a puppy socialiser for the first few months of their lives. Trainers give the dogs two sessions per day and the training lasts for about 16 weeks. Trainers work 9 to 5, Monday to Friday, but do some weekends on a rota. To become a hearing Dog Trainer requires a six-month course, followed by three months under supervision.

Kennel staff

The kennel staff care for the dogs being trained, paying attention to their health and husbandry. For more details on kennel work see Chapter 5.

Puppy socialiser

As with guide dogs, the first few months of a potential hearing dog's life is spent with a puppy socialiser. The aim of the job is to introduce the puppy to various experiences to produce a well-adjusted and confident dog that will be capable of fulfilling its role well. A placement is usually for six months. The charity covers the costs of veterinary fees, but puppy socialising is a volunteer position that is unpaid.

Dogs for the Disabled

Dogs for the Disabled train dogs to assist in tasks that able-bodied people take for granted. These include:

- opening and closing doors

- helping to maintain balance

- helping to get up after a fall

- fetching and retrieving

- bending and reaching tasks such as emptying a washing machine

- switching lights on and off.

Currently, dogs are trained by contracted-out GDBA Trainers. DFD also employs kennel staff and Puppy Walking Supervisors.

USEFUL ADDRESSES AND WEB SITES

Blue Cross, 1 High Street, Victoria, London SW1V 1QQ. Tel: (020) 7834 5556.

Cats' Protection League, 17 King's Road, Horsham, West Sussex RH13 5PN. Tel: (01403) 221900.

Dogs for the Disabled, The Old Vicarage, London Road, Ryton-on-Dunsmore, Coventry CV8 3ER. Tel: (01203) 302057. www.vois.org.uk/dftd

Donkey Sanctuary, Sidmouth, Devon EX10 0NU. Tel: (01395) 578222. www.vie.gla.ac.uk/donkey

Guide Dogs for the Blind Association, Hillfields, Burghfield Common, Reading RG7 3YG. Tel: (01189) 835555.

Hearing Dogs for Deaf People, London Road (A40), Lewknor, Oxford OX9 5RY. Tel: (01844) 353898. www.hearing-dogs.co.uk

International League for Protection of Horses, Anne Colvin House, Snetterton, Norfolk NR16 2LR. Tel: (01953) 498682. ilph@ilph.org

National Canine Defence League, 17 Wakley Street, London EC1V 7LT. Tel: (020) 8377 0006.

PDSA, Head Office, Whitechapel Way, Priorslee, Telford, Shropshire TF2 9PQ.

RSPCA, Head Office, Causeway, Horsham, West Sussex RH12 1HG. Tel: (01403) 264181. www.rspca.co.uk

SSPCA, Braehead Mains, 603 Queensferry Road, Edinburgh EH4 6EA. Tel: (0131) 3390222.

Wood Green Animal Shelters, Godmanchester, Huntingdon, Cambridge PE18 8LJ.

9

Working in Education and Research

TEACHING POSTS

Many jobs working with animals require some degree of teaching or training of others. This is because a lot of animal work is practical and on-the-job experience is essential. Some jobs require or recommend a qualification in education before taking on teaching roles. This may be the Certificate of Education (Further Education) or for those already possessing a degree, the Post Graduate Certificate of Education. However, requirements for a formal qualification vary widely, and details concerning the specific post should be sought.

Those considering teaching as an important part of their job should:

● be confident at lecturing and public speaking

● be proficient and experienced in the skills they wish to teach

● enjoy working with people

● be patient with slower learners.

Veterinary surgeon

Vets teach veterinary students voluntarily on the 'seeing practice' scheme (see Chapter 2). They also teach trainee veterinary nurses, although Qualified Veterinary Nurses also provide some of this training. Vets based in universities will also lecture students, and some specialist vets give continuing education lectures to qualified vets.

Veterinary nurse

Vet nurses teach trainee nurses, often helping them with practical skills such as bandaging. Many also play a role in teaching practical skills to vet students. Veterinary nurses also work in colleges, teaching veterinary nursing to trainees, by lectures and practical sessions.

Farriers

Since it is necessary to become an apprentice to a farrier before being able to practise farriery, many farriers will take on apprentices and teach them the ins and outs of the profession, while at the same time making use of the apprentice's slowly increasing skills.

Guide Dog Trainers

Qualified staff at the regional centres are responsible for teaching new Guide Dog Trainers.

Other teaching jobs

Other teaching jobs that may involve work with animals in a secondary capacity include:

- university lecturer (eg zoology)

- schoolteacher with responsibility for classroom pets

RESEARCH

There are many and varied opportunities to work with animals in a research capacity. However, if you are considering a career in this field, it is important to be aware of what the job constitutes, and to have carefully thought through your position on the ethics of the use of animals for research purposes.

Animals have been used to further medical research for centuries. In the past, animals have been used and abused with little regard for their welfare. From these experiments have come some great advances. For example, understanding the way in which the digestive system absorbs water took experiments that cost the lives of many rats, but from this a rehydration therapy was developed which has saved the lives of millions of people. On the other hand, some experiments have caused animal suffering with little or no benefit to people.

In recent years, public objection to animal experimentation has caused the introduction of tight rules concerning the use of animals for research. The government recently announced that no further licences would be granted to companies to use animals for researching the safety of cosmetics. To have a project licence for an experiment involving animals granted by the Home Office, an application is reviewed by a committee consisting of both scientists and non-scientists. The application is approved or rejected after weighing up the potential benefits against the possible suffering to the animal.

It should be emphasised that few experiments involve physical suffering to the animal. Many involve feeding of special diets or drugs to ensure they do not produce side effects, and of course, much research in the fields of conservation and zoology involves observing the animals in the wild, with virtually no effect on the animal at all.

Animals kept in research institutes are monitored closely by veterinary surgeons to ensure their welfare and health.

Scientific fields that may use animals as part of their research include:

- physiology

- zoology

- pharmacology

- medicine

- veterinary medicine

- psychology/ethology.

Research is usually carried out in universities that offer courses in those subjects. The route to enter research is by taking a relevant degree, which may involve some research projects, and then a PhD or other postgraduate qualification, which will usually be research orientated.

Private sector companies, particularly pharmaceutical companies, also have their own research departments and employ scientists in research capacities.

Besides those directing and performing the research, others are employed to care for and tend to the animals, as well as to monitor results.

Kennel staff

Institutions that house dogs and cats often employ kennel staff for general duties such as cleaning, feeding and minor healthcare tasks. See Chapter 5 for more information on kennel work.

Lab technician

Lab technicians often perform much of the routine animal husbandry and care of the laboratory animals. This includes such tasks as feeding, watering, cleaning out cages, kennels and runs and ensuring the animals are in good health. Lab technicians also assist researchers by taking measurements and observations which will help constitute the researcher's results. For example, this may mean making daily weight measurements or measuring food and water intake.

A wide variety of species are used in laboratory experiments. Common species used include:

● dogs

● cats

● rabbits and rodents

● primates.

After most experiments the animals are euthanased due to legal requirements, even if they have suffered no physical harm.

Laboratory work can often be routine, but can also be distressing, and it is necessary for the technician to steel him or herself against suffering and not get emotionally involved with the animals.

USEFUL ADDRESSES AND WEB SITES

Pfizer Limited, Sandwich, Kent CT13 9NJ. www.pfizer.co.uk
Bayer plc, Bayer House, Strawberry Hill, Newbury RG14 1JA.
www.bayer.co.uk

10

Working with Wild and Exotic Animals

This final chapter looks at some jobs that involve less familiar and non-domesticated species. Work with exotic and wild animals often permits little hands-on contact with the animals, since their lack of domestication makes them too shy or dangerous to handle. But the rewards of seeing some of these splendid animals in their natural environments (or as near a natural environment as can be provided), and helping to ensure their welfare, can be great in themselves.

ZOO KEEPER

Job description
Zoo keepers look after the animals kept in zoological collections and safari parks. There are about 300 zoos, safari parks, aquaria and bird collections in the UK. The largest of these are:

- Bristol

- Chester

- Edinburgh

- London

- Paignton

- Twycross

- Whipsnade

- Woburn.

The job involves the general care and husbandry of the animals kept in the collection. Species are often drawn from all round the world, and individual animals have widely varying requirements, such as for temperature, diet and humidity. It is also important to provide a varied and interesting environment (environmental enrichment), particularly for higher mammals and primates. It has become increasingly recognised over the years that animals' psychological as well as physical needs must be catered for. For example, a social animal needs the company of its own kind, a burrowing animal needs soil or sand so it can exhibit burrowing behaviour. Animals as diverse as chimps and polar bears benefit, both in their mental and physical health, from the addition of toys to their environment.

Zoo keepers' duties involve attention to all aspects of the welfare and health of the animals in their care. This means mucking out and cleaning, food preparation, feeding and watering. The keeper also monitors temperature and humidity, records feeding behaviour and health, and treats minor ailments or summons a vet when necessary. Another important task is to make sure all fencing is secure.

Keepers often have contact with the public, answering questions, particularly at feeding time, but also monitoring to make sure people do not behave irresponsibly, endangering either the animals or themselves.

The work is occasionally dangerous, some animals being deliberately aggressive and others such as elephants being capable of causing great damage accidentally. Dangerous animals are usually dealt with by keepers working in pairs, one of whom may be armed. Keepers in safari parks patrol, ensuring public safety, for example in case of breakdown, and monitoring the animals at the same time.

Working hours are usually longer from April to October. A five- to six-day week is usual, and it is sometimes necessary to work weekends and bank holidays on a rota.

What qualifications and experience are needed?

There are no set entry requirements, but preference is often given to applicants with three to five GCSEs at grade A to C, including English, maths and a science. As with many other jobs working with animals, competition for places is fierce. There are about 1,500 people working as zoo keepers in the UK. Often employers keep a list of applicants. It is important to gain experience working with animals before applying. General experience, such as in veterinary practices, is helpful, but it may be possible to get experience in a zoo on a voluntary basis.

Zoo keepers need to be enthusiastic about animals and conservation. They need to be physically fit – many of the duties involve hard labour. It is also important to have good interpersonal skills, and an ability to interact patiently and helpfully with people of all ages. A driving licence is essential for safari park work.

Training is on the job, coupled with a correspondence course for the City and Guilds Certificate in Zoo Animal Management (C+G 7630). This course consists of studying units, assignments and a project, and takes two years to complete.

Job prospects

It is usually possible with experience and the right qualities to progress to section leader or even head keeper, although the latter is often primarily a management job. Pay varies, and is usually fairly low, but sometimes subsidised accommodation is provided.

COUNTRYSIDE RANGER

Job description

Countryside wardens or rangers are employed by the land-owning authority, for example the Forestry Commission, to care for the countryside and the flora and fauna it contains. Duties vary, but usually involve an element of working with the public, advising good places to visit and areas to avoid that may be dangerous. Sometimes it is necessary to prevent damage or littering by specific people, and on rare occasions the police may have to be summoned.

There is also much maintenance work, such as fencing, picking up litter, keeping paths in good repair and managing woodland, for example by planting trees and clearing scrub. The work is often heavy and physical.

Rangers and wardens will often be involved in ecological or conservation work. A large part of this involves surveys, for example of badger trails or birds' nesting sites. By working out number and species of wildlife inhabiting an area, the land can be managed to specifically cater for the indigenous fauna's needs.

Rangers may also help in rescue work and emergencies such as fire or flood.

What experience and qualifications are needed?
Academic qualifications are not always necessary, but applicants for positions often have relevant examinations such as degrees or NVQs in subjects such as Land and Environment or Conservation Management.

Experience working on estates or in forestry is useful. Failing this, voluntary conservation work and evidence of an interest in the countryside are important. Training is usually on the job and organised by employers, with some external courses available. Subjects covered include:

- first aid

- map-reading

- countryside law

- fire-fighting.

Job prospects
There are only approximately 1,000 jobs for wardens and rangers in the UK, with healthy competition for places. A promotion structure is usually in place, allowing the possibility of rising to District Ranger or Head Warden. Starting salary is between £7,500 and £10,000, rising to £19,000 with experience. Officially working hours are 37 to 40 per week, but in practice are often longer and may involve weekend work.

PET SHOP ASSISTANT/MANAGER

Job description
Pet shops vary in size from the corner shop selling pet food, toys and a few goldfish, to the superstores such as Petsmart which sell a huge range of pet care equipment and stock a variety of animals and birds. Garden centres often have a pet section as well.

It is generally frowned upon nowadays to sell puppies and kittens in pet shops, since they are best left with their mothers until rehomed, and potential buyers prefer to see the rest of the litter with the mother. Animals that are commonly found in pet shops include:

- rabbits

- hamsters, gerbils, rats and mice

- budgerigars and canaries

- coldwater and tropical fish

- reptiles.

The pet shop worker thus needs an understanding of the correct conditions and diet necessary for this wide range of species, both to keep them healthy while in the shop, and to be able to advise new owners as to their care.

There is a large element of working with the public, giving health care advice and helping owners to decide which pets are suitable for their own particular circumstances. Other duties include regular cleaning of cages, feeding and checking for signs of ill health, as well as general shop duties such as manning the cash register and cleaning and tidying. In addition, the pet shop manager or owner is responsible for stocking levels, employees, and other general management and administrative tasks.

What qualifications and experience are needed?
No specific qualifications are necessary, but experience of general work with animals such as in a veterinary practice is useful. N or SVQs in Animal Care also give an advantage.

Job prospects
Large stores will have their own promotion scales. Promotion opportunities in smaller stores are limited, but work in a pet shop can be a useful stepping stone to other jobs like kennel work or veterinary nursing.

USEFUL ADDRESSES AND WEBSITES

Association of British Wild Animal Keepers, c/o Luke Gates, Chessington Zoo, Leatherhead Road, Chessington, Surrey KT9 2NE.

British Trust for Conservation Volunteers, 36 Saint Mary's Street, Wallingford, Oxon OX10 0EU. Tel: (01491) 839766.

English Nature, Northminster House, Peterborough PE1 1UA. Tel: (01733) 340345.

Federation of Zoological Gardens of Great Britain and Ireland, Zoological Gardens, Regent's Park, London NW1 4RY.

Whipsnade Wild Animal Park, Dunstable, Bedfordshire. www.londonzoo.co.uk/whipsnade

Appendix 1

University and College Courses

UNIVERSITIES OFFERING VETERINARY NURSE TRAINING

University	Courses offered
Bristol University	BSc, Veterinary Nursing and Practice Administration
University of West England, Bristol	BSc or HND, Veterinary Nursing Science
University of Central Lancashire	BSc or HND in Veterinary Nursing, HND in Veterinary Practice Management
Middlesex University	BSc, Veterinary Nursing
University of Plymouth	HND, Veterinary Nursing and Management

UNIVERSITIES OFFERING AGRICULTURAL DEGREES

University	Courses offered
University of Aberdeen	BScAgri, Agriculture
University of Wales, Aberystwyth	BSc or HND, Agriculture
Askham Bryan College	HND, Agriculture
University of Wales, Bangor	BSc, World Agriculture
Bishop Burton College	HND, Agriculture
University of Central Lancashire	HND, Agriculture
University of Derby	HND, Organic Agriculture

The University of Edinburgh	BSc, Agriculture
Harper Adams University College	BSc or HND, Agriculture BSc, International Agriculture BSc or HND, Farm Management
University of Newcastle Upon Tyne	BSc, Agriculture BSc. Farm Business Management
The University of Nottingham	BSc, Agriculture
Nottingham Trent University	HND, Agriculture
University of Plymouth	BSc, Agriculture BSc, Agriculture and Countryside Management BSc, Food Production and Quality
Queen's University of Belfast	BAgr, Agriculture
University of Reading	BSc, Agriculture
Scottish Agricultural College	HND, Agriculture
Sparsholt College Hampshire	HND, Agriculture-Production and Management
Writtle College	BSc or HND, Agriculture
Wye College	BSc, Agriculture

Appendix 2

Training and Starting Salaries

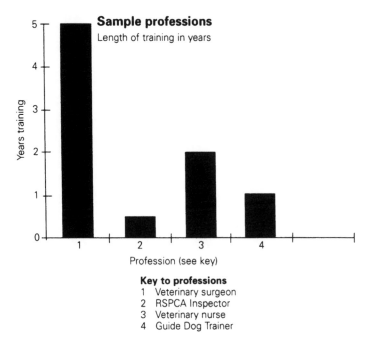

Fig. 5.   Sample professions and length of training.

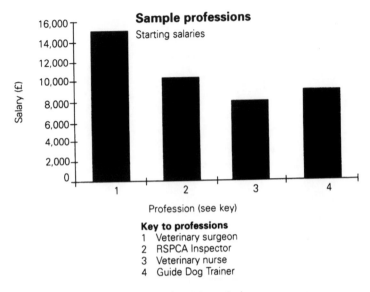

Fig. 6. Sample professions and starting salaries.

Glossary

Brucellosis. A disease of cattle, potentially transmissible to humans.

Calving. The process of a cow giving birth to a calf.

Clostridia. A group of bacteria, one example of which causes tetanus.

Dehorning/disbudding. Removing the horns from adult cattle, or the horn buds from calves.

Electrocardiogram (ECG). A graphical reading of the heart's activity.

Ethology. The study of animal behaviour.

Euthanasia. Humane destruction.

Farrowing. The process of a sow giving birth to piglets.

Food conversion ratio. The efficiency of a farm animal at turning feed into produce.

Friesian. A breed of dairy cow.

Gastro-intestinal. Pertaining to the stomach and intestines.

Husbandry. The general care of animals, literally the business of a farmer.

Internal fixation. A method of repairing fractured bones using internally placed pins, plates and screws.

Lambing. The process of a ewe giving birth to a lamb.

Laminitis. A foot disease of horses.

Metritis. An inflammatory, usually infectious, disease of the womb.

Pasteurella. A bacterium often associated with pneumonia.

Post mortem examination. Examination of a body or carcass after death, to determine the cause of death, or ensure that the carcass is free from disease.

Radiography. The science of taking x-rays.

Radiology. The science of interpreting x-rays.

Ragwort. A common plant that is particularly poisonous to horses.

Runt. The smallest in a litter, and least likely to survive.

Index

WORKING WITH DOGS
How to spot the jobs and get qualified for them

Pauline Appleby

'Recommended reading for anyone who wants to work with dogs . . . a great fund of information of jobs available, qualifications you will need and how to go about getting the right training and experience.' *Your Dog.* 'Invaluable information for school leavers and mature job hunters – the only available handbook of its kind.' *Kennel and Cattery Management.*

128pp. illus. 1 85703 468 6. 2nd edition.

WORKING WITH HORSES
How to get the right qualifications, training and job opportunities

Jenny Morgan

Racing stables, riding schools, studs, rescue organisations, eventing yards, the army – the opportunities for working with horses seems almost limitless. You could become a groom, jockey, yard manager, trainer, equestrian journalist, or vet, in the UK or abroad. Whatever your dream, this in-depth guide details the many possibilities, and outlines the necessary experience and qualifications, if any. Don't keep wondering if you could work with horses – read this book and find out! Jenny Morgan is a well-known equestrian journalist and experienced producer of show horses.

96pp. illus. 1 85703 561 5. 2nd edition.

WORKING FOR THE ENVIRONMENT
How to make a career of caring for the world we live in

Barbara Buffton

'[A] detailed and impartial overview of all types of work in the UK environmental/countryside sector. [It] is the most comprehensive account I have come across and covers the Who, What, Where, When, How and Why of the most important career in the world.' *Niall Carson, Countryside Jobs Service.* 'Covers courses, jobs and careers available throughout the environmental industry.' *The Job Hunter's Guide.*

144pp. illus. 1 85703 366 3.

WORKING IN THE VOLUNTARY SECTOR
How to find rewarding work with charities and voluntary organisations

Craig Brown

Whatever your age or skills, whether you want to work full time, part time, or just a few hours a week, this invaluable guide tells you what you need to know. 'Packed with accessible information and written from the author's years of experience and recruitment in the voluntary sector . . . suitable for Year 11 upwards, and adults considering this kind of work' *Newscheck.* '. . . describes the benefits of working for a charity and the different types of work available – be it paid or unpaid in the UK or overseas.' *Streetwyse.*

136pp. illus. 1 85703 367 1.

3511350R00070

Printed in Great Britain
by Amazon.co.uk, Ltd.,
Marston Gate.